# BaptistWay Adult Bible Study Guide®

# 14 Habits of Highly Effective Disciples

ELLIS OROZCO
ALICE STEGEMANN
BYRON STEVENSON
DENNIS WILES

BaptistWayPress®
Dallas, Texas

BAPTISTWAY PRESS® Leadership Team
Executive Director, Baptist General Convention of Texas: David Hardage
Director, Church Ministry Resources: Chris Liebrum
Director, Bible Study/Discipleship Team: Phil Miller
Publisher, BaptistWay Press®: Scott Stevens

Cover and Interior Design and Production: Desktop Miracles, Inc.
Printing: Data Reproductions Corporation

First edition: June 2014
ISBN–13: 978–1–938355–17–2

# How to Make the Best Use of This Issue

Whether you're the teacher or a student—

1. Start early in the week before your class meets.

2. Overview the study. Review the table of contents and read the study introduction. Try to see how each lesson relates to the overall study.

3. Use your Bible to read and consider prayerfully the Scripture passages for the lesson. (You'll see that each writer has chosen a favorite translation for the lessons in this issue. You're free to use the Bible translation you prefer and compare it with the translation chosen for that unit, of course.)

4. After reading all the Scripture passages in your Bible, then read the writer's comments. The comments are intended to be an aid to your study of the Bible.

5. Read the small articles—"sidebars"—in each lesson. They are intended to provide additional, enrichment information and inspiration and to encourage thought and application.

6. Try to answer for yourself the questions included in each lesson. They're intended to encourage further thought and application, and they can also be used in the class session itself.

If you're the teacher—

A. Do all of the things just mentioned, of course. As you begin the study with your class, be sure to find a way to help your class know the date on which each lesson will be studied. You might do this in one or more of the following ways:

  • In the first session of the study, briefly overview the study by identifying for your class the date on which each lesson will be studied. Lead your class to write the date in the table of contents on page 9 and on the first page of each lesson.

- Make and post a chart that indicates the date on which each lesson will be studied.
- If all of your class has e-mail, send them an e-mail with the dates the lessons will be studied.
- Provide a bookmark with the lesson dates. You may want to include information about your church and then use the bookmark as an outreach tool, too. A model for a bookmark can be downloaded from www.baptistwaypress.org on the **Adults— Bible Studies** page.
- Develop a sticker with the lesson dates, and place it on the table of contents or on the back cover.

B. Get a copy of the *Teaching Guide,* a companion piece to this *Study Guide.* The *Teaching Guide* contains additional Bible comments plus two teaching plans. The teaching plans in the *Teaching Guide* are intended to provide practical, easy-to-use teaching suggestions that will work in your class.

C. After you've studied the Bible passage, the lesson comments, and other material, use the teaching suggestions in the *Teaching Guide* to help you develop your plan for leading your class in studying each lesson.

D. Teaching resource items for use as handouts are available free at www.baptistwaypress.org.

E. Additional Bible study comments on the lessons are available online. Call 1–866–249–1799 or e-mail baptistway@texasbaptists.org to order *Premium Adult Online Bible Commentary.* It is available only in electronic format (PDF) from our website, www.baptistwaypress.org. The price of these comments for the entire study is $6 for individuals and $25 for a group of five. A church or class that participates in our advance order program for free shipping can receive the *Premium Adult Online Bible Commentary* free. Call 1–866–249–1799 or see www.baptistwaypress.org to purchase or for information on participating in our free shipping program for the next study.

F. Additional teaching plans are also available in electronic format (PDF) by calling 1–866–249–1799. The price of these additional teaching plans for the entire study is $5 for an individual and

$20 for a group of five. A church or class that participates in our advance order program for free shipping can receive *Premium Adult Online Teaching Plans* free. Call 1–866–249–1799 or see www.baptistwaypress.org for information on participating in our free shipping program for the next study.

G. You also may want to get the enrichment teaching help that is provided on the Internet by the *Baptist Standard* at www.baptiststandard.com. (Other class participants may find this information helpful, too.) The *Baptist Standard* is available online for an annual subscription rate of $10. Subscribe online at www.baptiststandard.com or call 214–630–4571. (A free thirty-day trial subscription is currently available.)

H. Enjoy leading your class in discovering the meaning of the Scripture passages and in applying these passages to their lives.

## Do you use a Kindle?

This BaptistWay *Adult Bible Study Guide* plus *Guidance for the Seasons of Life; Living Generously for Jesus' Sake; Profiles in Character; Psalms: Songs from the Heart of Faith; Amos, Hosea, Isaiah, Micah; Jeremiah and Ezekiel; The Gospel of Matthew; The Gospel of Mark; The Gospel of Luke: Jesus' Personal Touch; The Gospel of John: Part One; The Gospel of John: Part Two; The Book of Acts: Time to Act on Acts 1:8; The Corinthian Letters: Imperatives for an Imperfect Church;* and *Hebrews and the Letters of Peter* are now available in a Kindle edition. The easiest way to find these materials is to search for "BaptistWay" on your Kindle or go to www.amazon.com/kindle and do a search for "BaptistWay." The Kindle edition can be studied not only on a Kindle but also on a PC, Mac, iPhone, iPad, Blackberry, or Android phone using the Kindle app available free from amazon.com/kindle.

## AUDIO BIBLE STUDY LESSONS

Do you want to use your walk/run/ride, etc. time to study the Bible? Or maybe you're looking for a way to study the Bible when you just can't find time to read? Or maybe you know someone who has difficulty seeing to read even our *Large Print Study Guide*?

Then try our audio Bible study lessons, available on *Living Generously for Jesus' Sake*; *Profiles in Character*; *Amos, Hosea, Isaiah, Micah*; *The Gospel of Matthew*; *The Gospel of Mark*; *The Gospel of Luke*; *The Gospel of John: Part One*; *The Gospel of John: Part Two*; *The Book of Acts*; *The Corinthian Letters*; *Galatians and 1 & 2 Thessalonians*; and *The Letters of James and John*. For more information or to order, call 1–866–249–1799 or e-mail baptistway@texasbaptists.org. The files are downloaded from our website. You'll need an audio player or phone that plays MP3 files (like an iPod®, but many MP3 players are available), or you can listen on a computer.

# Writers for This Study Guide

**Dennis R. Wiles** wrote **lessons one through four.** Dennis is the pastor of First Baptist Church in Arlington, Texas. He was reared in a Christian home in Birmingham, Alabama by faithful parents. He has attended Baptist churches his entire life. He has two degrees from Southwestern Baptist Theological Seminary. He is married to Cindy, the love of his life, and they have two children and two grandchildren.

**Alice Stegemann** wrote **lessons five through seven.** Alice has taught Sunday School for over thirty years. A graduate of Southwestern Baptist Theological Seminary, she has both written and edited Bible study materials for teenagers. Alice gave her life to Christ while praying alone in her bedroom just before her twelfth birthday. She and her husband Jack live in Hendersonville, Tennessee.

**Ellis Orozco** wrote **lessons eight through eleven.** Dr. Orozco is the pastor of First Baptist Church in Richardson, Texas. He has a degree in engineering from Texas A&M University, an M.Div. from Southwestern Baptist Theological Seminary, and a D.Min. from Truett Seminary at Baylor University. Ellis has served as pastor at Corpus Christi Baptist Church and at Calvary Baptist Church in McAllen, Texas. He has served on numerous committees for the Baptist General Convention of Texas and is currently on the board of Buckner International. He is married to Priscilla and they have three children.

**Byron Stevenson** wrote **lessons twelve through fourteen.** He is senior pastor of The Fort Bend Church in Sugar Land, Texas. He is a graduate of Southern University, Baton Rouge, Louisiana, with a Bachelor of Science in Accounting, and he also earned a Master of Arts in Theological Studies from Houston Baptist University. Byron has served in a variety of roles with the Baptist General Convention of Texas and was elected first vice president of the convention for 2012. Pastor Stevenson is married to Tonya and they have two daughters.

# 14 Habits of Highly Effective Disciples

# Introducing

# 14 Habits of Highly Effective Disciples

## Approaching This Study of
## 14 Habits of Highly Effective Disciples

There is much discussion today on the state of disciple-making in the evangelical church in America. Virtually all denominations are reporting declining membership numbers. Southern Baptists recently reported that their baptism numbers (baptism being the first step of discipleship beyond conversion) for 2012 had dipped to levels not seen since 1948. These statistics are particularly sobering when we consider that the population in the U.S. continues to grow.

While there are certainly many contributing factors to the discipleship deficit in our churches, what can be done about it? Perhaps a renewed focused on what it means to be a disciple could be helpful. A disciple is basically a learner or follower. Webster includes the following definition: "one who accepts and assists in spreading the doctrines of another."[1] We have been called to be followers of Christ and have been commissioned (Matthew 28:18–20) to make disciples of all nations. We have also been called to grow in our faith. So, what should be some distinguishing practices of those who have chosen to be disciples of Christ?

This study will address fourteen habits that should be a regular part of the life of a disciple. It is important to understand that these habits are not practiced to earn God's favor (can't be done—salvation is by grace through faith alone), but are actually faith in action (1 Timothy 4:7–8)—motivated by the great love God has shown us in Jesus. Make no mistake—they do require action—activity that should grow out of our identity in Christ and our pursuit to follow him.

Perhaps that is part of the discipleship challenge. It is easier to espouse correct belief than it is to act on it. Unfortunately, discipleship cannot be automated and disciples cannot be produced in a microwave. Disciple-making is a time-consuming process—both for the teacher and the learner. The good news is that we have resurrection-power available to us through the Holy Spirit to guide and teach us on our discipleship journey.

This study of *14 Habits of Highly Effective Disciples* is part of our annual summer emphasis on studying a biblical theme. For a complete list of our studies see www.baptistwaypress.org.


## Studying These Lessons

Regular physical check-ups are an important part of a healthy lifestyle. While we may not always enjoy these close encounters with our physicians, these regular appointments can prevent problems and improve our quality of life. Regular spiritual check-ups are also a necessary part of a growing disciple's life. They provide us with an opportunity to evaluate our growth and commitment, and can serve as motivation for increased faithfulness in our witness and service.

This study on the habits of disciples can serve as a spiritual check-up for our lives. The habits to be studied are not a complete list, but they provide a good baseline for measuring our spiritual health. Take advantage of this study and use it as a guide to evaluate the current state your spiritual health. Pay particular attention to the Main Idea and Study Aim for each lesson. Seek to move beyond a simple acknowledgement of the main idea to actually applying the truth as a spiritual habit in your life. As you approach each lesson, pray and ask God to reveal the health of that particular habit in your life and be prepared to make adjustments as necessary.


## The Nature of Habits

Habits are funny things. They can be positive or negative. They can bring us closer to God or push us further away. They can be acquired through repetition (many suggest it takes twenty-one days to create a habit) but they can also become an automatic characteristic, or even "An established disposition of the mind or character."[2] That's what we need—to establish a settled disposition in both our mind and character that is focused on Jesus.

The best part is: *we get to choose the habits that become a part of our lives.* As disciples of Jesus Christ, we can choose to form habits in our lives that express our faith. The Bible provides us with encouragement and examples that can lead us to be more effective followers of Christ. May these lessons help us to evaluate our spiritual habits and lead us to choose to grow as faithful disciples of our Lord.

### 14 HABITS OF HIGHLY EFFECTIVE DISCIPLES

| | | |
|---|---|---|
| Lesson 1 | Bible Study | Psalm 119:9–16; Acts 17:10–12; 2 Timothy 3:14–17 |
| Lesson 2 | Confession | Psalm 51; 1 John 1:9 |
| Lesson 3 | Faith | Proverbs 3:5–6; Galatians 2:15–21; Ephesians 2:8–10 |
| Lesson 4 | Fasting | 2 Chronicles 20:1–4, 13–15; Matthew 6:16–18; Acts 13:1–3 |
| Lesson 5 | Fellowship | Acts 2:42–47; Romans 12:3–13 |
| Lesson 6 | Love | Proverbs 17:17; 1 John 4:7–21 |
| Lesson 7 | Obedience | 1 Samuel 15:1–35 |
| Lesson 8 | Prayer | Luke 11:1–13; 18:1–8 |
| Lesson 9 | Purity | Psalm 24:1–6; Ephesians 5:1–16 |
| Lesson 10 | Service | Mark 10:35–45; John 13:12–16; James 2:14–17 |
| Lesson 11 | Stewardship | Deuteronomy 8:10–18; Matthew 25:14–30 |
| Lesson 12 | Thankfulness | Psalm 103; Luke 17:11–19 |
| Lesson 13 | Witnessing | Romans 10:8–15; 1 Corinthians 15:1–8 |
| Lesson 14 | Worship | Isaiah 6:1–8; Revelation 4:1–11 |

## Additional Resources for Studying
*14 Habits of Highly Effective Disciples*[3]

Kenneth L. Barker and John R. Kohlenberger III. *The Expositor's Bible Commentary—Abridged Edition: New Testament*. Grand Rapids, Michigan: Zondervan, 1994.

Bruce Barton, Philip Comfort, Grant Osborne, Linda K. Taylor, and Dave Veerman. *Life Application New Testament Commentary*. Carol Stream, Illinois: Tyndale House Publishers, Inc., 2001.

Dietrich Bonhoeffer. *Discipleship. Dietrich Bonhoeffer Works, Volume 4*, General Editor: Wayne Whitson Floyd, Jr. Minneapolis: Fortress Press, 2003.

Francis Chan. *Multiply: Disciples Making Disciples*. Colorado Springs, CO: David C. Cook, 2012.

Leroy Eims. *The Lost Art of Disciple Making*. Grand Rapids: Zondervan, 1978.

Richard J. Foster. *Celebration of Discipline: The Path to Spiritual Growth—Third Edition*. New York: HarperCollins Publishers, 1998.

Kyle Idleman. *Not a Fan: Becoming a Completely Committed Follower of Jesus*. Grand Rapids, MI: Zondervan, 2011.

Craig S. Keener. *IVP Bible Background Commentary: New Testament*. Downers Grove, Illinois: InterVarsity Press, 1993.

Eugene Peterson. *A Long Obedience in the Same Direction: Discipleship in an Instant Society*. Downers Grove, Illinois: InterVarsity Press, 1980.

David Platt. *Follow Me: A Call to Die. A Call to Live*. Carol Stream, IL: Tyndale House Publishers, Inc., 2013.

A.T. Robertson. *Word Pictures in the New Testament: Concise Edition*. Nashville, Tennessee: Holman Bible Publishers, 2000.

Donald S. Whitney. *Spiritual Disciplines for the Christian Life*. Colorado Springs, CO: NavPress, 1991.

Dallas Willard. *The Spirit of the Disciplines: Understanding How God Changes Lives*. New York: HarperCollins Publishers, 1988.

Spiros Zodhiates and Warren Baker. *Hebrew-Greek Key Word Study Bible, New International Version*. Grand Rapids, Michigan: Zondervan, 1996.

# NOTES

1. *Merriam-Webster's Collegiate Dictionary, Eleventh Edition,* Springfield, MA: Merriam-Webster, Inc., 2007, 356.

2. http://www.thefreedictionary.com/habits

3. Listing a book does not imply full agreement by the writers or BAPTISTWAY PRESS® with all of its comments.

## FOCAL TEXTS

Psalm 119:9–16;
Acts 17:10–12;
2 Timothy 3:14–17

## BACKGROUND

Psalm 119:9–16;
Acts 17:10–12;
2 Timothy 3:14–17

## MAIN IDEA

Disciples read, study,
memorize, and live
out God's word.

## QUESTION TO EXPLORE

How can I grow in my
knowledge and application
of God's magnificent word?

## STUDY AIM

To develop a plan to increase
the depth, quality, and
consistency of my study and
application of biblical truth

## QUICK READ

We will not become strong
and mature disciples
accidentally. One of the
necessary ingredients in
the recipe for spiritual
growth is the knowledge and
direction gained through the
disciplined study of the Bible.

# LESSON ONE
# *Bible Study*

## Introduction

When I began my ministry as a pastor, the Lord was gracious enough to allow me to pastor rural churches. The first two churches I served were filled with farmers and cattlemen. I didn't realize what a blessing that was at the time. I learned so much from those folks.

A deacon-farmer in one of those churches took me out on his land one morning. We were talking about his work and how much he enjoyed it. Our conversation quickly turned to a spiritual discussion of how God provided the land, minerals, seeds, and water for the farm. However, the farmer turned to me during that conversation and said, "Preacher, I do thank God for all he does for me. But he has never plowed my field or taken the seed out of the barn and planted it for me. I have to meet him halfway."

That was a powerful spiritual insight! Just like God doesn't sow seeds for the farmer, he doesn't force knowledge on us. You and I have to "meet him halfway" like my theologian/farmer friend said. We need spiritual truth, for sure. However, if we are going to learn and live as effectively as possible, we have to study the Bible for ourselves.[1]

## PSALM 119:9–16

[9] How can a young man keep his way pure? By living according to your word. [10] I seek you with all my heart; do not let me stray from your commands. [11] I have hidden your word in my heart that I might not sin against you. [12] Praise be to you, O LORD; teach me your decrees. [13] With my lips I recount all the laws that come from your mouth. [14] I rejoice in following your statutes as one rejoices in great riches. [15] I meditate on your precepts and consider your ways. [16] I delight in your decrees; I will not neglect your word.

## ACTS 17:10–12

[10] As soon as it was night, the brothers sent Paul and Silas away to Berea. On arriving there, they went to the Jewish synagogue. [11] Now the Bereans were of more noble character than the

Thessalonians, for they received the message with great eagerness and examined the Scriptures every day to see if what Paul said was true. ¹² Many of the Jews believed, as did also a number of prominent Greek women and many Greek men.

## 2 TIMOTHY 3:14–17

¹⁴ But as for you, continue in what you have learned and have become convinced of, because you know those from whom you learned it, ¹⁵ and how from infancy you have known the holy Scriptures, which are able to make you wise for salvation through faith in Christ Jesus. ¹⁶ All Scripture is God-breathed and is useful for teaching, rebuking, correcting and training in righteousness, ¹⁷ so that the man of God may be thoroughly equipped for every good work.

## God's Word is Worth It (Psalm 119:9–16)

Psalm 119 is an acrostic. Each stanza represents a letter from the Hebrew alphabet as the psalmist is praising God's word "from a to z." Our focal text for today is taken from the second stanza where the psalmist expressed his joy in knowing and applying God's truth to his life (Psalm 119:14). Obviously, the only way to apply God's truth to life is to know God's truth in the first place!

In verse 11, we are reminded of the power of memorization. God's word is truth and our minds need to be shaped by truth. As we memorize passages from the Bible, we are soaking our conscious and unconscious minds with truth. Jesus said, "Then you will know the truth, and the truth will set you free" (John 8:32). Memorizing takes time and energy, but it is worth it. Some people claim they can't memorize Scripture. My response to that is—you can if you want to! Think about it. We memorize Social Security numbers, phone numbers, lists of passwords, birthdays, lyrics from songs, poems, grocery lists, people's names, addresses, zip codes, etc. We have an amazing capacity for memorization.

Spiritual formation also requires the discipline of meditation (Ps. 119:15). Meditation means to consider, mull over, cogitate, and reflect on truth. It is not the "emptying" of the mind as some have suggested. In the Bible, this word means to saturate your mind with truth. It is both necessary and valuable to take time to reflect and contemplate on truth from Scripture.

As we are in the process of memorizing and learning to meditate on Scripture, we must meaningfully apply it to our lives. The psalmist made the connection between learning truth and applying truth. Notice the result of memorizing Scripture—". . .that I might not sin against you" (119:11). He also challenged the reader to purity by living according to God's word (119:9). Further, he rejoiced as he followed God's commands in his own life (119:14).

There is nothing like God's word. His word is worthy of our energy spent in memorizing, meditating, and meaningfully applying it to our lives. The path toward spiritual maturity is paved with the disciplined study and application of biblical truths. God's word is powerful and is

## HELPFUL ATTITUDES FOR BIBLE STUDY

What kind of person makes a good Bible student? Here are some attitudes to emulate to assist you in becoming a good student of God's word:

1. Spiritually hungry—Jesus said we are blessed if we hunger and thirst for righteousness (Matthew 5:6).

2. Receptive to God's truth—we need to be open-minded and yielded in our spirit to hear God's truth fully.

3. Devoted—studying the Bible will require time and effort. It is not easy.

4. Obedient—when God reveals truth to us, we need to implement it right away.

5. Disciplined—making time for study will require strong will and diligence to the process of learning. It is like learning any other difficult skill. However, just like a trained pianist is "free" to play the piano, we can also be "free" to live the life God has planned for us.

able to accomplish his purposes in our lives (Hebrews 4:12). As disciples, we should hunger and thirst for the wisdom of God revealed through his word.

Interestingly, the psalmist used the phrase "I have hidden your word in my heart" (119:11a). However, God's word was revealed through his behavior (119:9, 14). Hiding God's word in our hearts leads to behavior that is consistent with his word. So, in fact, hiding God's word is one sure way of making its truths known in and through our lives!

## Go to Class! (Acts 17:10–12)

Paul and Silas were directed by God to travel to Macedonia to share the good news about Jesus (Acts 16:9–10). They set sail immediately and finally arrived in Philippi. This was predominantly a Roman military city in the first century and there was no synagogue. Paul and Silas shared the gospel with Lydia and her family and they believed and were baptized. After spending time in Philippi, they made the 100 mile journey to the port city of Thessalonica, the largest city in Macedonia. At some point they preached in the synagogue there and were forced to leave. From there they traveled the three-day (fifty mile) journey to Berea. After arriving, as was their habit, they entered the synagogue and began to teach.

Luke points out that the Bereans were "of more noble character" (17:11) than the Thessalonians. This was revealed by the behavior of the people of Berea. They ". . . received the message with great eagerness and examined the Scriptures every day . . ." (17:11). The Greek word for "examine" (*anakrino*) came from the legal system in the first century. It meant to investigate thoroughly without bias. These Jews in Berea were willing to take an unbiased approach to Paul's teaching and compared it to the Scripture.

Ever since the time this record was provided by Luke, people who are open to God's word and are willing to study its truth impartially have been referred to as "Bereans." We can learn from their example. It is easy to simply make decisions about truth based upon our opinion or experience. We may realize our opinions are more influenced by worldly philosophy than the truths of God's word!

We are without excuse in regard to the opportunity to examine the truths of Scripture for ourselves. We live in a free society where access to good, sound biblical teaching is readily available. Our major metropolitan areas are amply supplied with Christian bookstores filled with Bible studies and helps. The Internet is home to innumerable sources that can assist any Bible student in their journey of Scriptural study.

The Bible is a library of truth waiting to be discovered by diligent students. You can familiarize yourself with its literary genres and its styles of expression. Again, it takes effort to study the Bible. As a senior in college, I enrolled in a particularly difficult course taught by a professor who was well known to be a challenging instructor. On the first day of class he acknowledged the difficulties associated with both him and the course. He offered us some sound, simple advice: "Come to class!" I would encourage you to "go to class" as a Bible student. You will have to study, but it will be worth your effort.

## Study and Live! (2 Timothy 3:14–17)

Paul began his second missionary journey from Antioch with Silas as his mission partner (Acts 16:40). While visiting the Galatian town of Lystra, Paul became acquainted with Timothy, son of Eunice and grandson of Lois (Acts 17:1–3; 2 Timothy 1:3–7). He decided to invite Timothy to accompany his team on its missionary journey. Timothy was both Greek and Hebrew and thus, would prove useful to Paul in the task of preaching and teaching about Jesus in the multicultural context of the first century. Timothy proved himself to be a faithful ministry partner and became an influential leader in the early church.

After writing Timothy a letter during his first imprisonment in Rome (1 Timothy), Paul sent him another letter from Rome during his second imprisonment (2 Timothy). Our passage today is found in this second letter where Paul challenged Timothy to be a "man of God" who was "thoroughly equipped for every good work" (2 Timothy 3:17). How could that happen to Timothy (or anyone for that matter)?

Paul admonished Timothy to continue the journey of learning that had characterized his life in Christ (3:14). He also reminded him of his family's commitment to biblical truth and how vital this had been to his own salvation (3:15).

In 2 Timothy 3:16–17, Paul made one of the most comprehensive statements about Scripture in the entire Bible. He described the nature

# HELPFUL HABITS FOR GOOD BIBLE STUDENTS

In order to develop as disciples, we must implement healthy study habits and practices that will enhance our learning journey.

1. Start with prayer. Ask the Holy Spirit to reveal God's truth to you.
2. Make sure you have a readable translation of the Bible.
3. Focus on the biblical text. Often we rely too much on study aids. Study the Bible first, before consulting commentaries or other study tools.
4. Choose a method of study. For example: book studies, word studies, character studies, thematic studies, theological studies, etc.
5. Take notes.
6. Utilize the work of reputable scholars.
7. Live out what you are learning. Invest in accountable relationships in your church. You need each other!

of Scripture as "God-breathed" (v. 16). This word hearkens back to the story of creation where God's breath contained creative authority, ". . . and God said . . ." (Genesis 1:3–30). We can also easily make the connection to John's revelation of Jesus as the Word of God (John 1:1, 14). The Scripture is the very "word" of God, revealed by his breath. This is a powerful word image for the normal English translation of "inspired."

Owing to the unique nature of Scripture, it is uniquely useful as well. Scripture reveals the wisdom and purposes of God. Paul proclaimed the practical nature of this God-breathed word—it is useful for ". . .teaching, rebuking, correcting and training in righteousness. . ." (2 Tim. 3:16).

"Teaching" implied the need for God's people to be taught the truth. The Bible contains the truths of God and thus, it should be taught to his people. "Rebuking" indicated God's need to address false doctrine and poor theology. "Correcting" is a word that referred to behaviors that need to change. "Training in righteousness" is an overarching idea that means God's word can help his people live upright and holy lives.

The result of the serious study and application of the God-breathed truth of Scripture is that the man of God can be appropriately equipped for God's service (v.17). Paul used the word "man" in the generic sense. We all have the responsibility as disciples to study and apply the truths of God's word to our lives.

## Implications and Actions

This lesson challenges us to be responsible for our own learning as disciples of Jesus Christ. God has revealed himself through his word. His word is readily available to us through modern translations of the Bible. Further, we have adequate resource material to aid us in our journey of biblical discovery. We must make the commitment to study God's truths for ourselves as we seek to be spiritually formed, mature disciples. This will require time and energy. We have to be willing to make an investment to memorize Scripture and meditate on its powerful truths. We also have to implement what we are learning in our daily lives as we seek to follow Jesus.

## QUESTIONS

1. What do we learn from Psalm 119 about the role God's word can play in our lives?

2. How can we demonstrate openness to God's truth today as the Bereans did in Paul's day?

3. How are you seeking to learn and apply God's truths as revealed in the Bible?

4.  What are some ways you can improve your Bible study habits?

5.  What is more difficult: learning God's word or living God's word? Why?

NOTES ————————————————————————————————————

1.  Unless otherwise indicated, all Scripture quotations in lessons 1–13 are from the New International Version (1984 edition).

FOCAL TEXTS
Psalm 51; 1 John 1:9

BACKGROUND
Psalm 51; 1 John 1:9

MAIN IDEA
Disciples confess their sins
to God in order to receive
forgiveness and restoration.

QUESTION TO EXPLORE
How current and
comprehensive is the
confession of my sin?

STUDY AIM
To ask God to conduct a
spiritual check-up of my life
and to honestly confess my sin

QUICK READ
The completed work of Christ
secures our relationship with
him. However, our daily
fellowship with God is affected
by how we live. Confessing our
sins and repenting from them
enables us to maintain close
fellowship with our Father.

# LESSON TWO
*Confession*

## Introduction

One of my seminary professors shared this story with me years ago. He had agreed to the seminary policy that no professor would publicly criticize a colleague in class. In a weak moment, he joined with some students who were complaining about a fellow professor. He knew he had violated the policy and that he was wrong for publicly encouraging his students in their criticism.

He said he sat in his office that afternoon for a long time in silence. He confessed his sin to God and asked for forgiveness. He resolved to never do it again. He then began the long walk down the hall to his colleague's office. He went in to visit with his fellow professor and confessed what he had done. He asked for forgiveness and shared his commitment to never do it again.

He told me it was one of the hardest things he had ever done. Confession and repentance are hard. But the difficulty associated with these ancient practices makes them powerful reminders in our lives. Hopefully, once we have confessed our sin, repented, and made amends—we will never forget it and will emerge from the experience as transformed people.

# PSALM 51

[1] Have mercy on me, O God, according to your unfailing love; according to your great compassion blot out my transgressions. [2] Wash away all my iniquity and cleanse me from my sin. [3] For I know my transgressions, and my sin is always before me. [4] Against you, you only, have I sinned and done what is evil in your sight, so that you are proved right when you speak and justified when you judge. [5] Surely I was sinful at birth, sinful from the time my mother conceived me. [6] Surely you desire truth in the inner parts; you teach me wisdom in the inmost place. [7] Cleanse me with hyssop, and I will be clean; wash me, and I will be whiter than snow. [8] Let me hear joy and gladness; let the bones you have crushed rejoice. [9] Hide your face from my sins and blot out all my iniquity. [10] Create in me a pure heart, O God, and renew a steadfast spirit within me. [11] Do not cast me from your presence or take your Holy Spirit

from me. [12] Restore to me the joy of your salvation and grant me a willing spirit, to sustain me. [13] Then I will teach transgressors your ways, and sinners will turn back to you. [14] Save me from bloodguilt, O God, the God who saves me, and my tongue will sing of your righteousness. [15] O Lord, open my lips, and my mouth will declare your praise. [16] You do not delight in sacrifice, or I would bring it; you do not take pleasure in burnt offerings. [17] The sacrifices of God are a broken spirit; a broken and contrite heart, O God, you will not despise. [18] In your good pleasure make Zion prosper; build up the walls of Jerusalem. [19] Then there will be righteous sacrifices, whole burnt offerings to delight you; then bulls will be offered on your altar.

# 1 JOHN 1:9

[9] If we confess our sins, he is faithful and just and will forgive us our sins and purify us from all unrighteousness.

## A Cry for Mercy (Psalm 51:1–2)

Biblical scholars refer to the Psalms that deal with pleas for forgiveness as "penitential" psalms (e.g. Psalms 6, 32, 102, 130, 143). However, Psalm 51 is the most famous one in this category. In fact, the heading of this psalm points the reader to the historical setting for its composition. David committed adultery with Bathsheba and the prophet Nathan confronted him (2 Samuel 11–12).

This sordid tale was the most humiliating and embarrassing episode in the life of King David. He actually thought he had "gotten by" with it after Uriah (Bathsheba's husband) had died in battle (a death David arranged). He moved Bathsheba into the palace and she delivered a son from their adulterous affair. However, about a year after David had committed these sins, God confronted him through the prophet Nathan (2 Sam. 12). At some point after this confrontation, David penned Psalm 51.

The psalm opens with a desperate plea for God's mercy. In fact, David appealed to God's covenant love in verse 1 as the basis for God's merciful response to his actions. The comprehensive nature of David's offense is revealed in the vocabulary he chose to describe both his failure and the response he requested from God. Notice he used three different terms to describe his actions—transgressions, iniquity, and sin. He also used three different words to communicate his request—blot out, wash away, and cleanse.

## Honesty is the Best Policy (51:3–6)

David confessed in verses 3–6 that he had sinned against God. He admitted his transgression. He didn't seek to blame Bathsheba or anyone else. In his quiet moments, his sin was "always before him" (51:3). That is how it is sometimes for all of us. Before we ask God for his forgiveness, our sinful failures remain on our minds. Even if we think we have "gotten away" with something, we are still convicted by what we have done.

David was well aware of the fact that he had injured Bathsheba by his actions. Obviously, her husband Uriah was dead! However, David's ultimate sin was against God. David was the king. He was supposed to model a life of integrity and holiness for Israel. He was a political,

# THE $299.00 CONFESSION

Pete Rose was one of the greatest baseball players to ever play Major League baseball. He retired with the most base hits of any major leaguer. His record may never be broken. However, he is not in the Hall of Fame because he was banished from baseball due to his propensity for gambling. In particular, he has admitted he gambled on baseball while he was the manager of the Cincinnati Reds. As most people know, gambling is an "unforgivable" sin in baseball.

Rose has since apologized for his errors in judgment. In fact, he will send you a personal apology. He will send to any fan an autographed baseball that reads, "I'm sorry I bet on baseball." The catch is—you have to give him $299 to get the apology!

Confession is good for the soul. In fact, it is necessary for us to be healthy Christians. We don't do it so that we might profit from it, however. We do it because it is right and necessary.

military, and spiritual leader. He had failed in his duty. God's law had been abrogated and David took full responsibility for his actions.

Consequently, David understood that God was justified in his judgment. Even though he was pleading for mercy, he knew God should judge him for such a sinful lapse in judgment. He also acknowledged that God desires truth and transparency in our dealings with him (51:6). The word for "inmost place" in verse 6 is a word used to describe the practice of plugging water wells and sometimes secretly diverting their flow to keep them from being discovered by an enemy (2 Chronicles 32:30). So what does using this particular Hebrew word in this context teach us?

Our tendency is to "cover up" our misdeeds and to "hold back" an honest assessment of ourselves. It is easy to point out the inconsistencies in the lives of others, but we are often slow to admit the hypocrisy exhibited by our own sinful behavior. Jesus addressed this in the Sermon on the Mount (Matthew 7:3–5). David recognized God's desire was for him to be honest and open in his admission of guilt. Hiding (plugging up) or constructing barriers within ourselves is not the way to deal with sin. Openness and honesty is the path to restoration and healing.

## Life on the Other Side of Guilt (51:7–12)

Acknowledging our sin and admitting our struggle is not the full answer for our guilt. There are many people who have admitted their shortcomings and choose to continue in them. We have to take further steps and we need God's intervention to progress beyond our guilt. In verses 7–12, David asked God to bring about a renewal in his life.

The hyssop plant was used in ritual cleansing practices by priests in the ancient world. Hyssop is a plant belonging to the mint family and was recognized for its antiseptic qualities. The priests in Israel would take stalks from the plant and bind them together to form an anointing tool for ritual cleansing purposes. These stalks would be dipped in water and the water was sprinkled on both people and objects (Numbers 19:18–22). David asked God to perform this ritual over him. Obviously this was poetic language, but it indicated the desire David had for a complete purification process to rid him of his guilt.

As the process of restoration continues, we need to experience the freedom and refreshment that accompanies God's forgiveness in our lives

(Acts 3:19). David longed to be renewed and refreshed by God's expression of mercy. He asked God to restore his joy in spite of the crushing nature of his failure (Ps. 51:8). He asked God to give him a pure heart and to restore his spirit (51:10). Any of us who has honestly dealt with sin understands the need for this request. Perhaps David was weary from carrying the burden of his wrongdoing. He needed a fresh start. He longed for a new day. He needed new resolve. He needed a purified heart and a cleansed will. He asked God for help in ushering in a new day in his life.

David lived in a time before the Holy Spirit indwelt God's people. He had a real fear that God would abandon him in his sinful condition (51:11). He asked God to remain with him and bring back the joy of his salvation. When we are languishing in our sin and its attendant guilt, we lose our joy. David understood the reality of joyless living. He was ready for life beyond his guilt!

## Restored and Useful (51:13–19)

Can we still be useful to God after we have failed him? Praise God, we can! Notice David's insight in Psalm 51:13. He could be used to teach others who had transgressed as well. His life could become a testimony of God's grace and redemption. Only through humility and honesty is this possible (Ps. 13–17). David understood God was interested in his heart, not just his performance of ritualistic worship (Ps. 51:16–17). Our confession and repentance must be heartfelt and true. Our actions always reveal the authenticity of our inner person. To experience God's refreshment and renewing work, we must be inwardly humble and contrite.

The good news is that we can become useful servants in God's hands even after episodes of failure. God does not discard us because we are broken. He specializes in restoration projects! We can be transformed by his grace, restored by his mercy, and energized for his service. This is truly good news!

## Walking in the Light (1 John 1:9)

In 1 John 1, the Apostle John challenged his readers to walk in God's light. Our journey as Christians is lived out in community with others who are walking in this same light. We have fellowship with God and with each other as we walk the narrow path mentioned by Jesus himself (Matt. 7:13–14). However, as all of us can attest, we will make mistakes along "The Way." What are we to do as Christians when we fail?

In 1 John 1:9 we read that confession is a New Testament practice as well. In fact, this verse offers us insight into the process of forgiveness and restoration God offers us as his children. The first step is to acknowledge our sin before God. We must first confess and agree with God about our sin. We must be willing to view our sin through his eyes. Once we recognize the truth that we have sinned, we then confess it to our Lord.

Notice John informed his readers that our Lord is both faithful and "just." He is righteous. He will not tolerate sin. He is holy and clean. He demands the same from us. Once we acknowledge and confess our sin, this passage teaches us what happens next. God's forgiveness is immediate. He forgives us when we honestly confess our sin before him. However, he then moves to purify us from our unrighteousness. This is a process. He forgives us immediately—but it may take a while to clean us up!

I remember an incident as a misbehaving child. It was a time when I was caught by my Mom in my mischief. I was covered head-to-toe in mud. I asked her for her forgiveness for disobeying her. She smiled and granted it immediately. But it took her about thirty minutes to remove the dirt and mud!

From a theological standpoint, we must acknowledge this verse addresses our *fellowship* with God, not our *relationship* with God. Our relationship with God rests securely upon the finished work of Christ on the cross. Once we are redeemed by his grace, we are securely his children forever. However, our daily fellowship with God fluctuates based on our obedience to him. We receive his forgiveness as his children so that our fellowship with him can be restored and renewed.

Our relationship with God is not threatened by our daily transgressions or our serious moments of failure. The blood of Jesus was shed on the cross for our sin. Our acceptance into the family of God is made possible by God's grace manifested through Jesus. But we can choose to be out of fellowship with our Father. This verse helps us understand the pathway to renewed intimacy with God in our daily life.

## Implications and Actions

All of us are sinners (Rom 3:23). We give in to temptation and disobey God. The key to an abiding, rich, and meaningful life with God is connected to what we do after we have sinned. Our willingness to be honest with both God and ourselves is crucial to a healthy spiritual life. We must cultivate the discipline of confession. God wants to forgive and restore us. He may not remove the consequences of our poor choices, but he can redeem us to live in them more effectively. He can renew our hearts. He can restore our joy. His cleansing and purifying power is real and effective. He can empower us to be cleansed, refreshed, and prepared for a life of greater effectiveness if we will honestly and humbly address our failures.

## QUESTIONS

1. Describe how David responded to Nathan's confrontation with him over his sin with Bathsheba. What did David's response reveal about him?

2. What happens when we honestly confess and repent? How does God respond?

3. What are barriers that keep us from being willing to be honest and open with God about our sinfulness?

4. What did you learn about the difference between our relationship with God and our fellowship with God?

FOCAL TEXTS
Proverbs 3:5–6;
Galatians 2:15–21;
Ephesians 2:8–10

BACKGROUND
Proverbs 3:5–6;
Galatians 2:15–21;
Ephesians 2:8–10

MAIN IDEA
Disciples come to Jesus
through faith and live by faith.

QUESTION TO EXPLORE
Have I come to Jesus through
faith and am I living by faith?

STUDY AIM
To take a step of faith towards
Jesus for salvation; or to take
the next step of faith in my
journey of surrender to his will

QUICK READ
We receive Christ by faith—
and we are to live by faith.
We place our trust in God for
salvation. We must also place
our trust in him daily as we
follow him in obedience.

# LESSON THREE
## *Faith*

## Introduction

I remember encountering a very difficult period in ministry. The church I was serving was divided over a controversial issue. I thought I knew what to do. I planned a few personal visits and scheduled a couple of meetings with different groups of people. I thought the sheer force of my personality and the respect for the office of the pastor would "win the day" for me. I was wrong. In fact, in every case, the situation worsened.

My wife finally asked me, "Have you really sought the Lord's wisdom and direction in all of this? Or, are you just doing what you think is the right thing to do?" Wow! I began seeking God directly. I personally and professionally discovered that "leaning on my own understanding" was not effective! When I turned to God and trusted him, my plans were surrendered to his plans. I began sensing his direction and I followed obediently. Thankfully, the outcome was drastically different!

## PROVERBS 3:5–6

[5] Trust in the LORD with all your heart and lean not on your own understanding; [6] in all your ways acknowledge him, and he will make your paths straight.

## GALATIANS 2:15–21

[15] "We who are Jews by birth and not 'Gentile sinners' [16] know that a man is not justified by observing the law, but by faith in Jesus Christ. So we, too, have put our faith in Christ Jesus that we may be justified by faith in Christ and not by observing the law, because by observing the law no one will be justified. [17] "If, while we seek to be justified in Christ, it becomes evident that we ourselves are sinners, does that mean that Christ promotes sin? Absolutely not! [18] If I rebuild what I destroyed, I prove that I am a lawbreaker. [19] For through the law I died to the law so that I might live for God. [20] I have been crucified with Christ and I no longer live, but Christ lives in me. The life I live in the body, I live by faith in the Son of God, who loved me and gave himself for me. [21] I

do not set aside the grace of God, for if righteousness could be gained through the law, Christ died for nothing!"

# EPHESIANS 2:8–10

[8] For it is by grace you have been saved, through faith—and this not from yourselves, it is the gift of God— [9] not by works, so that no one can boast. [10] For we are God's workmanship, created in Christ Jesus to do good works, which God prepared in advance for us to do.

## He Can Be Trusted (Proverbs 3:5–6)

The capacity for faith is hard-wired into our reality as human beings. We naturally trust. Think about it. Each day you prove this truth. You drive on your side of the road and trust others to do the same. You give your mail to a total stranger to deliver on your behalf. You receive a prescription from a physician and submit it to a pharmacist. You have not been present for the preparation of the medication—but you trust the manufacturer and the dispenser. You promptly take the medication—as an act of faith.

Faith is an operative reality in the spiritual realm as well. It is the means by which we demonstrate our trust in God and his purposes for our lives. Faith is laced with intellectual and spiritual certainty in God and his will. It is so important to God that he has declared that we can't please him without it (Hebrews 11:6).

Our lives are filled with choices and options. We make big and small decisions regularly. Where are we going to live? What job offer will we accept? What will we eat for dinner? Which movie are we going to see? Will I get married or not? Will I marry that person? Will we have children? Are we going to move to another city? How will we respond to the news from the doctor? Choices—we make them all the time.

On one hand, God has given us a brain and he expects us to use it. On the other hand, he is asking us to join him in what he is accomplishing on earth and for eternity. He is inviting us to know him and follow him. He is inviting us to a lifelong adventure of faith. How will we answer him?

Proverbs 3:5–6 is a passage that is germane to this discussion. Here we read about the possibility of being totally surrendered to God every day. Notice God is inviting us to enjoy his wisdom and direction for our lives rather than having to rely on our limited perspective. Regardless of how bright we may be, we are still limited in what we know. Our understanding of any situation is limited by our human condition.

Here is the good news from Proverbs—God has made his wisdom available to us! He wants to direct our paths. He wants to lead us in his ways. This is available for us if we ask for it! We have to make a whole-hearted commitment to him. We must be willing to open every area of our lives to his direction. Notice the text reads, "acknowledge him" in "all" our ways. This means we are to submit our plans, ideas, challenges, decisions, and hearts to him. We are to place our will on the altar to be exchanged for his will.

If we make this kind of commitment, he responds by making our "paths straight" (3:6). This verse means God will direct us. He will guide us. He will lead us. He will oversee our decisions. He will give us promptings. He will bring the right circumstances to us so we can sense his will. He will surround us with the right influences to assist us. He will make himself known to us so we will understand his purposes.

We don't have to lean on our limited perspective. We don't have to only draw from our supply of experience. We can actually benefit from the incredible wealth of God's wisdom. He can be trusted. He is all-knowing. His will is always best. His plan is the right plan. His desires are the best desires.

## Take the First Step (Galatians 2:15–21)

Learning to trust God with all of our hearts begins by taking the first step of faith. Our tendency as human beings is to trust our instincts and base our decisions upon what makes sense to us. This seems to be logical on the surface. However, in reality this is a major mistake. We need to seek God first. We need to build our lives on his truth.

Paul addressed this human tendency in Galatians 2:11–21. There were leaders in some of the Galatian churches who sought to participate in their own salvation. Some of them felt that observing the Jewish laws and rituals was mandatory for eternal salvation. The idea that human effort was necessary seemed to make sense to them. In fact, even the Apostle Peter struggled for a season with this dilemma.

Notice in Galatians 2:11, Paul shared an encounter he had with Peter about this very issue. Paul reminded Peter that salvation in Christ was through faith and not through the observance of religious activity. In those early days of Christianity the leaders of the churches were grappling with the doctrine of salvation. The main question was, "What is salvation?" A further question was, "What does it take to be saved?"

Most of the early followers of Jesus were Jews. They accepted Jesus as the Messiah and decided to follow his teachings. However, as the movement began to grow, some of the followers of Jesus began to proclaim the gospel to Gentiles as well. This created an inevitable confrontation over the nature of salvation. Did these Gentiles need to convert to Judaism first? After all, wasn't Jesus the Jewish Messiah? Wasn't the observation of these ancient religious laws required for anyone who wanted to find salvation in Jesus?

Paul led the effort in the early church to define salvation. He argued that Jesus had fulfilled the requirements of the Jewish law and that his followers had been set free from religious regulations. As grateful as the

## FAITHFUL MAN MAKES FAITHLESS CHOICE

In Genesis 15:1–6, God engaged in a memorable exchange with Abraham. God promised to bless Abraham with an heir. He further promised that his family would grow into a multitude (Gen. 15:5). He had already promised Abraham that all the families of the world would be blessed through his family (Gen. 12:1–3). Abraham was a man of faith and he believed God (Gen. 15:6).

However, as time passed, it seemed as if God had forgotten the promise he had made to Abraham. In Genesis 16:1–4, Abraham and Sarah decided to "lean on their own understanding" and take matters into their own hands. You know the story. At Sarah's beckoning, Abraham had a son through her maidservant, Hagar. This son, Ishmael, was not the son of promise. Abraham and Sarah made a huge mistake by making this decision. In some ways, the world today remains influenced by that fateful choice.

Even a man as great as Abraham "leaned on his own understanding." What can we learn from his choice?

Jews needed to be for their legacy, the Messiah had come and everything had changed! Paul made this argument in Galatians 2:15–16. Salvation was not shackled by the law. Justification is a word derived from the legal system of the first century. It was a word that was used to describe a person who was declared "innocent" of all charges. That person was "justified."

So—how does a person become "justified" in the spiritual sense? By observing religious rituals? No! Paul declared justification was achieved by faith (Gal. 2:15–16). This was the first step. Placing faith in Jesus would lead to being justified in God's eyes. This act launches a lifetime of trusting in Christ. It leads to a total transformation of character. Placing faith in Christ opens the possibility of defeating the fleshly desires of the sinful nature and reflecting the very person of Jesus (Gal. 2:20).

In our world, people still want to somehow "contribute" to or "earn" their salvation. They want to believe their goodness or pious religious exercises will somehow please God. This is faulty thinking. The first step to pleasing God is to place your faith in Jesus Christ for the salvation of your soul! Observing religious rituals will not accomplish eternal salvation. Only by placing faith in Jesus can one experience eternal life.

## Accept the Gift (Ephesians 2:8–10)

In Paul's letter to the Ephesians, he takes up this topic as well. This was a circular letter intended not just for the Ephesian church—but also for the churches in the region around Ephesus. It was a general letter, not one in which Paul was addressing a problematic situation. Instead he was free to explain the complexity of salvation and the nature of the church. It is truly a literary masterpiece.

In Ephesians 2:8–10, Paul offered one of the clearest explanations of salvation found anywhere in Scripture. In no uncertain terms, Paul refuted any idea that human effort is involved in accomplishing salvation. Notice in verse 8, Paul declared that our salvation is rooted in and offered through the grace of God. What is grace? It is the unmerited favor of God. It is a gift from God. We cannot earn his grace, nor do we deserve his grace. His offer of grace speaks more of who he is than who we are. He is a God of grace. He extends the offer of salvation to humanity—but only through Christ.

Notice in verse 9 Paul ruled out the effectiveness of religious observance in the process of salvation. Our salvation is not the result of works! We can't earn our position in eternity. It is granted to us through God's favor. We cannot boast of any salvific accomplishment. God gets the glory for the salvation of human beings.

What is our role in salvation? We are to accept the gift by faith. God offers us grace and we are to respond in faith. We believe God and take him at his word. We accept his plan for forgiveness and eternal life. Our journey of faith begins with the first step of accepting God's gift. Then what happens?

Notice verse 10. God has provided us a lifetime of usefulness and purpose. He has declared we are his "workmanship" (*poiema* in Greek—can mean "masterpiece"). He has uniquely transformed us by his grace to live a life of faith. As we serve him daily, we are walking in the life of works he has custom-designed for us. We are not saved *by* works, we are saved *for* works. He hasn't redeemed us just for eternity—he has redeemed us to live purposefully here on the earth!

## Implications and Actions

God offers us a life of discovering and experiencing his will. He makes his wisdom available to us. He has made himself available to us as we face the complex decisions and challenges of our day. However, this life is only possible if we accept God's offer of salvation through Jesus Christ. We must place our faith in him and accept this grand offer. Once we receive the gift of eternal life, we then have the ability to walk by faith each day. We have the opportunity to seek his counsel and accomplish his purposes in our everyday lives. Faith is the integral ingredient of this lifelong journey: necessary at the beginning, along the way, and until we reach our final destination. We begin by trusting God and we live by trusting God.

## QUESTIONS

1. How difficult is it to refrain from leaning on your own understanding? What are some examples from your life where you have chosen to just trust your instincts rather than God's direction?

2. What is your understanding of salvation? What does it mean to be saved?

3. How would you define "grace"?

4. What are some evidences of "living by faith" in your life today? How are you following God's will for your life?

# LESSON FOUR
## *Fasting*

**FOCAL TEXTS**
2 Chronicles 20:1–4, 13–15;
Matthew 6:16–18; Acts 13:1–3

**BACKGROUND**
2 Chronicles 20:1–17;
Matthew 6:16–18; Acts 13:1–3

**MAIN IDEA**
Disciples fast to seek God
and his purposes.

**QUESTION TO EXPLORE**
Is God leading me to fast (from
food or anything else) in order
to seek him and his purposes?

**STUDY AIM**
To practice fasting (from food
or anything else) in order to
seek God and his purposes

**QUICK READ**
Fasting is both biblical and
practical and should be
practiced in the church today.

## Introduction

"I just don't think fasting is good for you." "My doctor would never let me fast." "Isn't fasting something that those cults are doing nowadays?" "I have to eat—I could never fast." I have heard all of these comments through the years from well-meaning Christians. In fact, I have even heard from some who worried that fasting for three days would lead to certain death!

Once after preaching on fasting, a concerned mom approached me after the service and said, "Our son has decided to fast because of your sermon. I hope you're happy!" Who knew this could be such a controversial topic?

In the biblical passages for this lesson, we have the opportunity to address fasting holistically and practically. The practice of fasting itself is not mysterious at all, though the ramifications and results of fasting may be shrouded in mystery.

## 2 CHRONICLES 20:1–4, 13–15

[1] After this, the Moabites and Ammonites with some of the Meunites came to make war on Jehoshaphat. [2] Some men came and told Jehoshaphat, "A vast army is coming against you from Edom, from the other side of the Sea. It is already in Hazazon Tamar" (that is, En Gedi). [3] Alarmed, Jehoshaphat resolved to inquire of the LORD, and he proclaimed a fast for all Judah. [4] The people of Judah came together to seek help from the LORD; indeed, they came from every town in Judah to seek him.

[13] All the men of Judah, with their wives and children and little ones, stood there before the LORD. [14] Then the Spirit of the LORD came upon Jahaziel son of Zechariah, the son of Benaiah, the son of Jeiel, the son of Mattaniah, a Levite and descendant of Asaph, as he stood in the assembly. [15] He said: "Listen, King Jehoshaphat and all who live in Judah and Jerusalem! This is what the LORD says to you: 'Do not be afraid or discouraged because of this vast army. For the battle is not yours, but God's.'"

## MATTHEW 6:16–18

[16] "When you fast, do not look somber as the hypocrites do, for they disfigure their faces to show men they are fasting. I tell you the truth, they have received their reward in full. [17] But when you fast, put oil on your head and wash your face, [18] so that it will not be obvious to men that you are fasting, but only to your Father, who is unseen; and your Father, who sees what is done in secret, will reward you.

## ACTS 13:1–3

[1] In the church at Antioch there were prophets and teachers: Barnabas, Simeon called Niger, Lucius of Cyrene, Manaen (who had been brought up with Herod the tetrarch) and Saul. [2] While they were worshiping the Lord and fasting, the Holy Spirit said, "Set apart for me Barnabas and Saul for the work to which I have called them." [3] So after they had fasted and prayed, they placed their hands on them and sent them off.

### Surrounded and Scared (2 Chronicles 20:1–4, 13–15)

Have you ever felt "surrounded"? If so, you can identify with Jehoshaphat, king of Judah. For almost twenty-five years (871–848 B.C.) he ruled the kingdom of Judah successfully. He walked in the ways of King David and pleased God by ridding the land of polluted practices left over from his father's reign. Toward the end of his leadership in Judah, Jehoshaphat faced the greatest test of his reign as king.

We read in 2 Chronicles 20:1 that an alliance of armies organized and planned an attack on Judah. This powerful coalition of forces had crossed the Dead Sea and landed at En Gedi, about thirty-five miles south of Jerusalem. These armies hoped the king of Judah would feel threatened enough to engage them on this narrow plain in battle. They could use the sea to their advantage and place troops between the army of Judah and Jerusalem, thus weakening Jehoshaphat's military position.

Further, the armies from the east far outnumbered Judah's forces and Jehoshaphat knew his army was no match against such a mighty opponent (20:12).

What was the king's response? Notice verse 3—he was scared! The good news was that his fear prompted him to seek God's wisdom. Instead of convening a strategy session with his trusted military leaders, Jehoshaphat sensed a spiritual response was to be his people's only hope. He called on the entire nation to enter into a time of spiritual activity. In fact, he called for a national fast (20:3).

God's people were familiar with the practice of fasting. On the annual celebration of the Day of Atonement, all of Israel was called upon to fast (Leviticus 16:29–31). Fasting was the practice of abstaining from food for spiritual purposes. Jehoshaphat's people knew how to do it. They understood that fasting was a practical discipline that had spiritual implications. The normal time spent in food preparation and eating was given to prayer and reflection. The people redeemed the time spent on providing for a physical need in order to fulfill a deeper, spiritual need. They cried out to God to save them. Their willingness to deny their bodies was a sure sign of the serious nature of their request.

People began to assemble at the temple in Jerusalem. They fully understood the threat that lay thirty-five miles to the south. Finally, Jehoshaphat stood before them as their spiritual leader, much like Solomon had done years earlier when the temple was dedicated (2 Chron. 6:12–42). He led them in a time of corporate prayer and petition. Together, the people of God had fasted and prayed. Then, they waited.

Finally, the word of the Lord came through the prophet Jahaziel (20:14). God heard the pleas of his people and he responded to their time of prayer and fasting. He promised he would deliver them by fighting this battle himself (20:15–17).

For us today, we don't often connect our spiritual practices with our dilemmas. Sometimes we find ourselves "surrounded and scared" by our circumstances. We can follow the example of Jehoshaphat and turn to a spiritual activity that just might lead to wisdom and insight for the answers we need. Fasting is an ancient spiritual discipline that can prove to be spiritually and practically beneficial if we will take the time to engage in it.

## When You Fast (Matthew 6:16–18)

In Matthew 6:16–18, Jesus offered instructions to his disciples about fasting. Notice verse 16 where Jesus said, "When" you fast. He assumed his followers would fast. The phrasing of this text clearly indicates he was not talking about ceremonial fasts like the Day of Atonement (everyone was fasting on that day). He was giving instructions about personal fasting. His disciples were Jews who already knew how to observe the feasts and celebrations. He was leading them to a deeper understanding of spiritual disciplines. He was calling them beyond the legalistic and hypocritical displays of religiosity rampant in his day.

In this passage we can discover some keys to understanding the practice of fasting for our day. First of all, this is a spiritual discipline that we should engage in. It is not reserved for "super-spiritual" Christians.

---

### FASTING—ABSTAINING FROM FOOD FOR SPIRITUAL PURPOSES

There are examples in the Bible of fasting from things besides food (the use of olive oil as a lotion for the skin, for example), but the normal use of this word applies to food. Most times of fasting in the Bible do not include refraining from water.

*Types of Fasts in the Bible*

1. Regular fasts—fasting from food as directed by God (Matthew 6:16–18)

2. Partial fasts—fasting from certain types of foods (Daniel 1:12)

3. Absolute fast—fasting from both food and water (Esther 4:16)

4. Supernatural fast—fasting for an extended period of time without food or water (Deuteronomy 9:9)

5. Congregational fast—the church agreeing to fast together (Acts 13:1–3)

6. National fast—the entire nation called into a time of fasting (2 Chronicles 20:1–17)

7. Annual fast—the Day of Atonement (Leviticus 16:29–31)

This is an activity for all of us. Second, we are not to make a big show of it! People have always been tempted to parade their spirituality in front of others. Jesus specifically condemns this. Fasting is a private decision. Jesus instructed his followers to continue their normal hygiene practices as usual (6:17). In other words, don't use fasting as an occasion to prove to others how spiritual you are!

Jesus also made a connection between the practice of fasting and God's response. He expressed the truth that God pays attention to what we do. He responds to his people. God is not aloof or disinterested. God has provided spiritual activities for us that can benefit us during the challenging times in our lives. Fasting is a spiritual discipline that gets both our attention and God's attention.

Fasting is a personal decision. We need prayer support when we are fasting, so we can inform a handful of our close brothers and sisters in Christ about our intent to fast and pray. They can support us and pray for us during our time of fasting. However, we don't announce it to the world just so others will be impressed. We fast for spiritual reasons only. It is a spiritual exercise—not a weight-loss program!

## Fasting and Church Business Meetings (Acts 13:1–3)

In Acts 13:1–3, the church at Antioch was seeking for wisdom in respond-ing to the call of God. In Acts 11:19–21, Luke recorded this church's decision to share Jesus with both Jews and Gentiles in Antioch. Both Saul (Paul) and Barnabas joined the church in Antioch and became leaders in its mission. After a trip to Jerusalem to deliver a financial gift to the church there, Saul and Barnabas had returned home to Antioch to seek further direction for ministry.

On one occasion, the church was together in worship and God revealed his plan for missionary action. God decided to single out Barnabas and Saul (Paul) and to use them as the first official mission team from a local church. The gospel was to be proclaimed across the ancient world by Christian merchants, slaves, business owners, craftsmen, leading women, and artisans. However, God also prepared Saul and Barnabas to be missionaries sent out from their local church to launch the mission-ary movement of the church.

Notice in Acts 13:1–3 that the church in Antioch fasted. They were fasting and worshiping together. They heard God's instruction and

# GUIDELINES FOR FASTING

1. Fasting is a legitimate spiritual discipline for God's people today.
2. Fasting is to be done for spiritual purposes. It is not intended for weight-loss or for health reasons. Biblical fasting promotes sensitivity to God's voice, heightens our prayer lives, strengthens our resolve and/or assists us in discerning God's will.
3. Fasting is not to be regulated by legalism.
4. Fasting is not a means of displaying our piety to others.
5. Fasting is not a means of earning God's favor. We fast because God is leading us to do it.

*Suggestions for Fasting*

1. Determine the spiritual purpose for the fast. Why are you fasting? Are you addressing a specific spiritual need? Are you seeking God's will in a decision?
2. Decide on the nature and the duration of the fast. Are you going to fast from food? The Internet? Social media? Sports on TV? And—how long will you fast? If you are going to fast from food and water—the duration should not be more than 3 days, unless God has specifically directed you to do so. Your body can go for many days without food. You cannot survive for more than a few days without water.
3. Get prepared: mentally, physically, and spiritually. You need to be ready for the fast in order for it to be most effective. **You should consult your physician if you have any questions about your ability to fast from food.** Spend some time with God in prayer prior to the fast. Read about periods of fasting in the Bible. Consult writers like Richard Foster or Donald Whitney to gain some practical insights about fasting.
4. Solicit prayer support from key people who will pray for you and encourage you.
5. Use your time wisely. Use the time you would spend eating in prayer and reflection.
6. Record any significant insights in a journal. You are asking God for his direction. Take the time to record what he reveals to you during the time of your fasting.

received his challenge to surrender these two leaders for his mission. They responded with a period of further fasting and prayer (Acts 13:3). Finally, after some period of time, they laid hands on them and released them to the ministry of God to the peoples of the world.

This church did not realize how significant this decision would become! The people of God in Antioch were simply being obedient to God's direction for them. They made decisions based on God's wisdom. Their decisions were laced with spiritual practices and sensitivity. They prayed and fasted before deciding how to proceed. Through their obedience, the missionary effort of the church was launched and the first mission team was sent out to proclaim the gospel to the ancient world. Paul would become the greatest missionary of the church. God would use him to establish churches across the ancient world and lead him to write almost one-third of the New Testament! Through prayer and fasting, the church in Antioch established him in ministry and mission.

When was the last time your church prayed *and fasted* before a significant decision? Too often, we rush beyond spiritual practices in making decisions in our churches. Perhaps we rely too much on reason and common sense without consulting God for his direction. I'm sure it was difficult to surrender Paul and Barnabas to serve as missionaries. I can hear someone asking in that business meeting, "How are we going to support them?" Or, maybe, "We can't let them go. We need them here in Antioch at our church." But, after praying and fasting, this church obeyed God and the entire world has been blessed. Wow!

## Implications and Actions

This lesson challenges us on both personal and corporate levels. In other words, both we and our churches need to consider the value of spiritual exercises in our everyday lives. The practice of the spiritual discipline of fasting has played a vital role in the lives of God's people for centuries. Individuals, churches, and nations have all participated in this practice and the results are in: Fasting is a spiritual discipline that God uses to accomplish his purposes.

## QUESTIONS

1. How did God use the practice of fasting in the life of Judah and in the church at Antioch in today's passages?

2. What were the instructions of Jesus about the practice of fasting?

3. Have you ever fasted? How did God use it in your life to accomplish his purposes?

4. What are your concerns about fasting?

5. How do you think God might be able to use fasting in your life?

6. When and how can God use fasting in the life of your church?

**FOCAL TEXTS**
Acts 2:42–47; Romans 12:3–13

**BACKGROUND**
Acts 2:42–47; Romans 12:3–13

**MAIN IDEA**
Disciples experience the benefits and responsibilities of Christian fellowship.

**QUESTION TO EXPLORE**
Am I experiencing the full benefits and responsibilities of Christian fellowship?

**STUDY AIM**
To identify and embrace the full benefits and responsibilities of Christian fellowship

**QUICK READ**
The early church learned that living in relationship with Christ also meant living in relationship with each other. Paul gave the early believers practical advice on building relationships, explaining both the benefits and responsibilities.

# LESSON FIVE
## *Fellowship*

## Introduction

If you only had one hour to disciple a brand new Christian, what would you say? I had that exact challenge a few years ago when I met with a young lady in East Asia less than twenty-four hours after she had given her life to Christ. She had never been to church, had never known any other Christians, and had never seen a Bible until I handed her one. Her questions were mostly about how to live out her faith: What did God want her to do? How should she behave toward other people? Under the leadership of the Holy Spirit, I opened her Bible to one of the passages for today because it outlines—in concise, practical terms—how to live in fellowship with others.

# ACTS 2:42–47

[42] They devoted themselves to the apostles' teaching and to the fellowship, to the breaking of bread and to prayer. [43] Everyone was filled with awe, and many wonders and miraculous signs were done by the apostles. [44] All the believers were together and had everything in common. [45] Selling their possessions and goods, they gave to anyone as he had need. [46] Every day they continued to meet together in the temple courts. They broke bread in their homes and ate together with glad and sincere hearts, [47] praising God and enjoying the favor of all the people. And the Lord added to their number daily those who were being saved.

# ROMANS 12:3–13

[3] For by the grace given me I say to every one of you: Do not think of yourself more highly than you ought, but rather think of yourself with sober judgment, in accordance with the measure of faith God has given you. [4] Just as each of us has one body with many members, and these members do not all have the same function, [5] so in Christ we who are many form one body, and each member belongs to all the others. [6] We have different gifts, according to the grace given us. If a man's gift is prophesying, let him use it in proportion to his faith. [7] If it is serving, let him

serve; if it is teaching, let him teach; [8] if it is encouraging, let him encourage; if it is contributing to the needs of others, let him give generously; if it is leadership, let him govern diligently; if it is showing mercy, let him do it cheerfully. [9] Love must be sincere. Hate what is evil; cling to what is good. [10] Be devoted to one another in brotherly love. Honor one another above yourselves. [11] Never be lacking in zeal, but keep your spiritual fervor, serving the Lord. [12] Be joyful in hope, patient in affliction, faithful in prayer. [13] Share with God's people who are in need. Practice hospitality.

## The Life of the Church (Acts 2:42–47)

The coming of the Holy Spirit at Pentecost had just occurred. Three thousand new believers had joined the relatively small core group of Jesus' followers who had met to pray together in the days and weeks following his resurrection. Many of the new believers were not from Jerusalem; they had traveled from their homes to celebrate the Pentecost festival at the temple. These new Christians were probably reluctant to return home. There was so much to learn! And who better to learn from than the people who had been with Jesus during his earthly ministry?

Acts 2:42 provides a summary of those early days. The believers' activities were focused on four areas: teaching, fellowship, breaking of bread, and prayer.

The apostles had been taught by Jesus; they in turn passed on his teaching to those who had not had the blessing of hearing his words directly. Can you imagine all the wonderful stories that the apostles could tell that were *not* included in the written word? Remember too that these verbal accounts were the only source of information on Jesus' teaching at the time; the gospel writers had not yet begun their work of putting their memories and the memories of others down in writing.

The Greek word that is translated as "fellowship" in this verse is *koinonia*. It carries the idea of close association, relationship, and sharing. Most associations of people revolve around something the members have in common: nationality, profession, interests, etc. The early believers were a very diverse group, from all income levels and from multiple cultures and backgrounds. They didn't even share the same language. But there was one thing they had in common—they had faith in Jesus as their Savior. That was all they needed to bond together.

The "breaking of bread" could refer to either the observance of the Lord's Supper or to sharing meals together in each other's homes. Either way, the believers had the opportunity to engage in conversation and encouragement while nourishing their bodies. Think of some of the most meaningful conversations you have had in your life; how often were they over a meal?

Although the believers could have prayed together almost anywhere, it was quite possible they were meeting together in the temple area for prayer. They may have been continuing to honor the Jewish traditions. Also, the temple was a prime location for witnessing and sharing about their new faith.

The "everyone" of verse 43 probably included the community at large. The believers' neighbors were filled with reverential fear when they witnessed the apostles performing miracles.

Verses 44–45 paint a picture of a generous people. United by their love for God and each other, the early believers made sure that no one had an unmet need. Remember that many of the new believers were far from home and may have had difficulty earning a living to support their families in Jerusalem. Those Christians who had the means to support their spiritual brothers and sisters did so gladly.

Notice that verse 46 tells us that the believers met in two primary locations: the temple and in private homes. The temple provided a location where large numbers could gather at one time and where there was an opportunity to meet people seeking God. In individual homes, believers would have had more privacy in a relaxed setting and could indulge in longer conversations without being interrupted. These were times of worshiping and honoring God. God was blessing them with favor from their neighbors and with increasing numbers of new brothers and sisters in Christ.


## Life Relating to Others (Romans 12:3–8)

Paul's letter to the Romans divides itself into two major sections: Chapters 1–11 cover basic Christian doctrine, and chapters 12–16 explain how to live out those beliefs out in practical ways. After describing Christians as "living sacrifices" who are transformed and not conformed to the world, Paul explained the life of faith and fellowship with concrete examples.

There is nothing more poisonous to fellowship among believers than pride. Paul cautioned the believers in Rome to see their worth through God's eyes according to the gift of faith that had been given them (12:3). Having proper humility is a balancing act. Considering yourself worthless does not honor God or the value he has placed on your life by sending his Son to die for you. However, valuing your life over all others fails to recognize your debt to God's grace.

The human body is a fitting analogy for how believers are to relate to each other. Just as the body consists of a variety of limbs, organs, and systems—all serving different yet vital functions—so the church consists of a variety of believers with different gifts and functions that are vital to the health of the group as a whole (12:4–6). Paul listed seven gifts: prophesying, serving, teaching, encouraging, giving, leading, and showing mercy (12:6b–8).

Prophesying is not about telling the future; but rather is the gift of communicating God's message in a way that hearers can relate to. Although every Christian is called to serve, some are given a special gift for noticing and caring for the needs of others. Some believers are gifted with the ability to teach their fellow Christians the truths of the gospel.

## KOINONIA

The word *koinonia* means "fellowship, association, community, communion, joint participation, intercourse."[1] It describes more than a casual acquaintance; the term describes lives that are intimately bound together. If one member of the group hurts, everyone hurts. If one member rejoices, all rejoice. All members of the group are concerned with the physical and spiritual well-being of other members, being willing to share in any way they can. This fellowship is not dependent on sharing common traits; it transcends the social and cultural barriers that would keep people apart in a secular society. Believers share a common faith and a common Savior. They experience unity within their diversity.

But knowing those truths is not enough; those with the gift of encouraging can motivate others to apply those truths.

Some believers have the spiritual gift of knowing how and when to give their resources effectively. Christ had given new meaning to the idea of leadership; believers with the gift of leading are to use it to benefit those in their care, not to gain fame or fortune for themselves. The gift of showing mercy includes the ability to give help with the right attitude: with empathy and cheerfulness, not making the recipient feel worse about receiving the help.

No matter the gift, Paul reminded his readers that they were to practice each one wholeheartedly and humbly, with a spirit of gratitude for the privilege of contributing to the well-being of their fellow believers.

## A Life of Grace in Action (Romans 12:9–13)

Paul gave his readers suggestions for living out their faith in rapid fire succession in the next paragraph, thirteen ideas in all.

First, "Love must be sincere" (12:9). The word translated *sincere* means "without hypocrisy." Love is useless if it is faked. How many times have you experienced someone showering you with "affection," but you knew that he or she was only using you for their own purposes? Indifference would be easier to take! Without genuine, selfless love, the rest of the actions in the next few sentences would be worthless. (See 1 Corinthians 13:1–3.)

Paul called on his readers to hate evil (12:9b). The tense of the verb (along with most of the other verbs in this passage) suggests a continuing action. We are not just to hate one evil act; we are to practice a lifestyle of being disgusted by evil. Only when we have a visceral reaction to sin will we be motivated to fight against it.

Contrasted with our hatred of evil is our adherence to what is good. The verb translated "cling to" is used in other passages to describe the union between a man and a woman. We should be "married" to righteous living in a way that commands our utmost faithfulness.

"Devoted" describes the kind of love shared by parents and children; "brotherly love" denotes the love between siblings. The idea is that the relationship between believers should be as strong as the bond between

---

## DEVELOPING THE HABIT

Here are some ways to develop the habit of fellowship in your life:

- Look for opportunities to share meals with fellow church members, especially those who are struggling financially.
- Join or form a small group committed to praying together for the needs of your community.
- Seek to discover your own spiritual gifts and look for opportunities to practice them.

---

family members (12:10). This kind of relationship leads to putting the needs of our brothers and sisters in Christ above our own.

The word translated "zeal" carries with it the idea of speed. Have you ever had someone promise to provide you with assistance but delayed so long that the help was no help at all? The next phrase literally means "boiling in the spirit." We should be so eager to serve our fellow believers that we jump at the chance, recognizing that we are serving the Lord in the process (12:11).

Hope, for the Christian, is much more than wishful thinking; it is a confidence in the future because of Christ and what he has accomplished for the believer. As we set our mind on that hope, it brings joy. Our hope does not make us immune to problems, however. When trouble comes, we are to bear up under it with patience. And how can we focus on our hope and endure our troubles? We do so by persisting in regular prayer (12:12). Paul knew that believers could easily let the busyness of everyday activities crowd out time spent in prayer if they did not consciously make the effort to be faithful to fellowship with the Lord.

There were no government-sponsored "safety nets" in Paul's day. The poor were forced to beg or sell what few possessions they had—including sometimes their own freedom. Christians who had more than enough for their own survival were to share with those who were struggling, so all the believers could be free to serve the Lord without worrying about basic necessities (12:13).

Hospitality in those times was more than having a few friends over for dinner or a party. Travelers could find few suitable (and safe) places to stay. The believers who were willing to open their homes to strangers could provide them security and ease their anxieties. If the travelers were fellow believers, the hosts had the opportunity to form new relationships and to encourage others in their faith. If the travelers were not believers, what better witness to the love of Christ could the hosts demonstrate than to share everything they had?

## Implications and Actions

Discipleship does not occur in a vacuum. Some spiritual disciplines are developed privately, but we are created to need other human beings. Fellowship is a way to share knowledge and experiences and provide encouragement and support to fellow believers. It's about both giving and receiving, recognizing that we have a lot to learn—and have a lot we can teach. Fellowship can be harmed by pride; we should relate to our fellow believers with humility and sincerity. As we practice our gifts within the body of Christ, we have both the privilege and the responsibility to develop the bond of love within our spiritual family.

## QUESTIONS

1. Did the diversity of the early church make it stronger or weaker? Why?

2. Are you more likely to discuss your spiritual struggles in a classroom or at a dinner table? In which setting would you feel most comfortable sharing the spiritual insights you've gained?

3. What is the best way you've found to avoid unhealthy pride?

4.  What spiritual gift do you find the most opportunities to use?

5.  How can you practice genuine love? How can you avoid "faking it"?

NOTES ────────────────────────────────────────

1.  Koinonia. (2012). In *Enhanced Strong's Dictionary*—HCSB Study Bible (Version 5.1.8) [Mobile application software].

FOCAL TEXTS
Proverbs 17:17; 1 John 4:7–21

BACKGROUND
Proverbs 17:17; 1 John 4:7–21

MAIN IDEA
Disciples love others
because of God's example
and his command.

QUESTION TO EXPLORE
What keeps me from following
God's command to love others?

STUDY AIM
To decide how I will express
love to someone in the
coming week as a reflection
of my love for God.

QUICK READ
God's kind of love is not a
reaction to receiving affection
from someone else; his kind of
love is a decision to put another
person's needs above my own.

# LESSON SIX
## *Love*

## Introduction

Back in my college days I served as a summer missionary and I often led Backyard Bible Clubs. One of the most popular songs among the children had as its first verse, "Love is a flag flown high from the castle of my heart . . . for the King is in residence there." I would always explain the background of this song to the children: In England, a special flag is traditionally flown above the castle where the king or queen is residing. That way, the citizens in the surrounding area know their monarch is in their presence.

In the same way, love expressed in the life of a believer is evidence that the King of kings is residing in that person's life. The analogy may have been a little too abstract for the youngest participants to grasp, but it certainly stuck with me. How could others know that Jesus was in my life if the "flag" of love was not evident? "So let it fly in the sky, let the whole world know . . . that the King is in residence there."[1]

## PROVERBS 17:17

[17] A friend loves at all times, and a brother is born for adversity.

## 1 JOHN 4:7–21

[7] Dear friends, let us love one another, for love comes from God. Everyone who loves has been born of God and knows God. [8] Whoever does not love does not know God, because God is love. [9] This is how God showed his love among us: He sent his one and only Son into the world that we might live through him. [10] This is love: not that we loved God, but that he loved us and sent his Son as an atoning sacrifice for our sins. [11] Dear friends, since God so loved us, we also ought to love one another. [12] No one has ever seen God; but if we love one another, God lives in us and his love is made complete in us. [13] We know that we live in him and he in us, because he has given us of his Spirit. [14] And we have seen and testify that the Father has sent his Son to be the Savior of the world. [15] If anyone acknowledges that Jesus is the

Son of God, God lives in him and he in God. [16] And so we know and rely on the love God has for us. God is love. Whoever lives in love lives in God, and God in him. [17] In this way, love is made complete among us so that we will have confidence on the day of judgment, because in this world we are like him. [18] There is no fear in love. But perfect love drives out fear, because fear has to do with punishment. The one who fears is not made perfect in love. [19] We love because he first loved us. [20] If anyone says, "I love God," yet hates his brother, he is a liar. For anyone who does not love his brother, whom he has seen, cannot love God, whom he has not seen. [21] And he has given us this command: Whoever loves God must also love his brother.

## Love for a Friend (Proverbs 17:17)

This verse is one of many in Proverbs that gives us wise sayings about friendship. The Hebrew word translated "loves" carries the meaning of a strong attachment and warm feelings. Much like our English word *love*, this word is used throughout the Old Testament in a variety of situations: loving children, spouses, food, money, truth, and God's law. But it is also the word used to describe God's love for his people and the love we should have for God.

It is easy to love someone who makes you feel good or has something to offer you. Loving someone when he or she is cranky or sick is harder. But that is the measure of true friendship. A friend does not choose to love only when it is convenient or pleasant. Sometimes, however, loving a friend when he or she is experiencing success can be difficult as well because envy can creep in. Good times or bad, a true friend will consistently put your needs first and be willing to rejoice or mourn right along with you.

Is the mention of a "brother" intended to contrast or complement the steadfastness of a friend? Certainly friends can be as close as family members. But family members sometimes can be more persistent in their love and support during difficult times. Either way, we are reminded that love doesn't falter during rough times.

## Love from God (1 John 4:7–12)

In John's command to his readers to love one another, he echoed the words of Jesus (John 15:12). God is the Source of love and his love is our main motivation to love others. This kind of love is a result of our rebirth and our continued growth in the knowledge of God. The last part of verse 7 could be misunderstood; John was not saying that everyone who demonstrates any kind of love is a child of God. Because we are all created in the image of God, any human being has the ability to show love. Perhaps you know some nonbelievers who are good, loving people. But human love has its limitations; it can be fickle or artificial or motivated by self-interest. Only God's kind of love will endure.

If someone is incapable of the self-giving love that God has demonstrated to us, that person has proved that he or she does not know God (1 John 4:8). Knowing God necessarily changes us and our character. The more we experience God's love in our lives and learn about God's true nature, the more we want to be like him. People who do not have that experience are not motivated to reflect the same kind of love.

In the way that humans can sometimes twist logic, some have distorted the statement that "God is love" (4:8b) to mean that "love is God." The two statements do not mean the same thing. Love is so much a part of God's character that his very essence is love. Love colors everything he does. On the other hand, the concept of love, even at its noblest, cannot be the object of our worship.

Verse 9 closely parallels the more familiar John 3:16. The train of thought in both verses is, because God loved us, he sent his Son so that we might have eternal life through him. Note that in John 3:16, God loved the "world"; in 1 John 4:9, he "showed his love among us." The two phrases may not actually be that different in thought: God is able to demonstrate his love for the world through his children.

John reminded his readers in verse 10 that love didn't begin with them. They had not pled and begged for affection from a reluctant god who begrudgingly returned their affection. God loved us first, before we could even attempt to "earn" his favor. In fact, Scripture makes it clear that we *cannot* earn his love and we could never deserve what he has done for us.

The primary way that God has demonstrated his love for us is by making a way for us to be reconciled to him through the sacrifice of his

---

# AGAPE

Greek has a much richer distinction than English among the many shades of the meaning of love. *Eros* love is a physical attraction and describes the passion between a man and a woman. *Storgeo* is the natural love between family members, especially between parents and children. *Phileo* describes the kind of love between friends that is a result of fondness for each other and shared interests. *Agape,* on the other hand, is an act of the will more than it is an emotion. It is the kind of love you show toward someone who is unlovable and unlikely to return that love. This is the word used to describe the love that God extended to us while we were sinners and in rebellion against him, and it is the word used to describe the love we are expected to show to our fellow human beings.

---

Son. Any human act of love pales in comparison. In response, we can do no less than to love our brothers and sisters in Christ with a sacrificial love (4:11). One of the great privileges we have as children of God is to be the visible manifestation of his love. Because he lives in us, others can see God's love in action through our lives.

## Love Because of God (1 John 4:13–21)

Love for others is just one proof that God lives in us. The Spirit's presence in us is evidence that we are living in Christ (4:13). And because of the Spirit's empowering, we can be witnesses to the saving power of Jesus. Once again, we see echoes of John 3:16 in 1 John 4:14. God the Father has sent his Son to be the "Savior of the world."

Earlier in chapter 4, John discussed false prophets with the "spirit of the antichrist" (4:3) and how to discern them—only those who acknowledge that Jesus came in the flesh are truly speaking for God. Now in verse 15, we see the other side of the coin. Those who recognize Jesus as the Son of God are living in God. In 1 Corinthians, Paul similarly pointed out that only true believers could say that Jesus is Lord (1 Cor. 12:3). This is more than just an intellectual exercise; confessing that Jesus is the Son of God and that he is Lord means that we are following

## Developing the Habit

Here are some ways to develop the habit of love in your life:

- Strive to put yourself in someone else's shoes before judging their actions.
- Look for ways to encourage and help those who feel rejected by your community.
- Meditate on the love that God has shown to you.
- Be conscious of the times you make unkind comments about others and pledge to confine your remarks to positive, affirming comments.

him in obedience. We have personal experience with God's love and we "rely" on it (1 John 4:16).

Because God's love is perfected in us, we are like Christ in the love we show to the world. Ephesians 5:1 tells us to be "imitators" of God in the way we show love. Because of this, we do not need to dread Judgment Day. We can be confident that we will be judged in the light of our identity in Christ (1 John 4:17).

We should have a healthy fear of God, a respectful awe of him. But we don't have the kind of fear that worries about being punished, because we know God wants the best for us. Fear and love cannot occupy the same heart. In fact, love actively "drives out" fear (4:18). If we know someone loves us, we are not afraid of what that person might do to us. At the same time, if we love someone else, we are also not afraid of what he or she might do, because we have that person's best interest at heart.

In verse 19, John reminded his readers once again that God began the cycle of love. Our love is in response to his. But note that the response is not just a matter of reciprocating love to the One who loved us. God expects us to love those who may or may not love us back. This becomes a test of whether our love for God is genuine. Loving God and hating a brother are incompatible (4:20). Because we can't see God, it is possible for someone to pretend to love God and not be found out. But it is a lot harder to fake love for people who can be seen and who can sense insincerity. And as if to make his case even stronger, John reminded his readers that Jesus explicitly commanded us to love others (4:21).

## Implications and Actions

Love is the foundation on which all discipleship habits are built. If we cannot practice sincere love, all other activity is meaningless and can become a source of spiritual pride instead of a means of spiritual growth. Sincere love is not influenced by circumstances; we show love even—or especially—during difficult times. Just as God loved us when we were unlovely, we are to show love to those who may or may not return that love. Love is an act of the will and not just an expression of emotion. God is both the example and source of the love we show to others.

## QUESTIONS

1. Describe a time when a friend showed genuine love to you.

2. Why is it sometimes hard to show love?

3. Is it easier to show love when a fellow believer is experiencing success or failure? Why?

4. What are some signs that love is genuine? How can you develop those characteristics in your life?

NOTES ——————————————————————————

1. Anonymous, Public Domain.

# LESSON SEVEN
## *Obedience*

**FOCAL TEXT**
1 Samuel 15:1–35

**BACKGROUND**
1 Samuel 15:1–35

**MAIN IDEA**
Disciples choose to obey
God completely.

**QUESTION TO EXPLORE**
Do I choose to obey
God completely?

**STUDY AIM**
To choose to obey God
completely in every
area of my life

**QUICK READ**
Partial obedience or
conditional obedience is not
real obedience at all. God
expects our wholehearted
commitment to him
and his commands.

## Introduction

There is something in human nature that makes us resistant to being told what to do, even when we know it is for our best. Have you ever gotten a new appliance or electronic gadget with a complicated set of instructions? Perhaps you looked at the directions and said to yourself, "I don't need these; I can figure it out on my own." Then you struggled your way through, taking more time than reading the directions would have taken, and discovering that the device did not work as well as you thought it should. That's when you realized your pride had kept you from getting the best results. Sometimes we treat God's instructions that way. We foolishly think we know better than God how to accomplish his will. Saul, Israel's first king, fell into that same trap.

## 1 SAMUEL 15:1–35

[1] Samuel said to Saul, "I am the one the Lord sent to anoint you king over his people Israel; so listen now to the message from the Lord. [2] This is what the Lord Almighty says: 'I will punish the Amalekites for what they did to Israel when they waylaid them as they came up from Egypt. [3] Now go, attack the Amalekites and totally destroy everything that belongs to them. Do not spare them; put to death men and women, children and infants, cattle and sheep, camels and donkeys.' " [4] So Saul summoned the men and mustered them at Telaim—two hundred thousand foot soldiers and ten thousand men from Judah. [5] Saul went to the city of Amalek and set an ambush in the ravine. [6] Then he said to the Kenites, "Go away, leave the Amalekites so that I do not destroy you along with them; for you showed kindness to all the Israelites when they came up out of Egypt." So the Kenites moved away from the Amalekites. [7] Then Saul attacked the Amalekites all the way from Havilah to Shur, to the east of Egypt. [8] He took Agag king of the Amalekites alive, and all his people he totally destroyed with the sword. [9] But Saul and the army spared Agag and the best of the sheep and cattle, the fat calves and lambs—everything that was good. These they were unwilling to destroy completely, but everything that was despised and weak they totally destroyed.

<sup>10</sup> Then the word of the LORD came to Samuel: <sup>11</sup> "I am grieved that I have made Saul king, because he has turned away from me and has not carried out my instructions." Samuel was troubled, and he cried out to the LORD all that night. <sup>12</sup> Early in the morning Samuel got up and went to meet Saul, but he was told, "Saul has gone to Carmel. There he has set up a monument in his own honor and has turned and gone on down to Gilgal." <sup>13</sup> When Samuel reached him, Saul said, "The LORD bless you! I have carried out the LORD's instructions." <sup>14</sup> But Samuel said, "What then is this bleating of sheep in my ears? What is this lowing of cattle that I hear?" <sup>15</sup> Saul answered, "The soldiers brought them from the Amalekites; they spared the best of the sheep and cattle to sacrifice to the LORD your God, but we totally destroyed the rest." <sup>16</sup> "Stop!" Samuel said to Saul. "Let me tell you what the LORD said to me last night." "Tell me," Saul replied. <sup>17</sup> Samuel said, "Although you were once small in your own eyes, did you not become the head of the tribes of Israel? The LORD anointed you king over Israel. <sup>18</sup> And he sent you on a mission, saying, 'Go and completely destroy those wicked people, the Amalekites; make war on them until you have wiped them out.' <sup>19</sup> Why did you not obey the LORD? Why did you pounce on the plunder and do evil in the eyes of the LORD?" <sup>20</sup> "But I did obey the LORD," Saul said. "I went on the mission the LORD assigned me. I completely destroyed the Amalekites and brought back Agag their king. <sup>21</sup> The soldiers took sheep and cattle from the plunder, the best of what was devoted to God, in order to sacrifice them to the LORD your God at Gilgal." <sup>22</sup> But Samuel replied: "Does the LORD delight in burnt offerings and sacrifices as much as in obeying the voice of the LORD? To obey is better than sacrifice, and to heed is better than the fat of rams. <sup>23</sup> For rebellion is like the sin of divination, and arrogance like the evil of idolatry. Because you have rejected the word of the LORD, he has rejected you as king." <sup>24</sup> Then Saul said to Samuel, "I have sinned. I violated the LORD's command and your instructions. I was afraid of the people and so I gave in to them. <sup>25</sup> Now I beg you, forgive my sin and come back with me, so that I may worship the LORD." <sup>26</sup> But Samuel said to him, "I will not go back with you. You have rejected the word of the LORD, and the LORD has rejected you as king over Israel!"

[27] As Samuel turned to leave, Saul caught hold of the hem of his robe, and it tore. [28] Samuel said to him, "The LORD has torn the kingdom of Israel from you today and has given it to one of your neighbors—to one better than you. [29] He who is the Glory of Israel does not lie or change his mind; for he is not a man, that he should change his mind." [30] Saul replied, "I have sinned. But please honor me before the elders of my people and before Israel; come back with me, so that I may worship the LORD your God." [31] So Samuel went back with Saul, and Saul worshiped the LORD. [32] Then Samuel said, "Bring me Agag king of the Amalekites." Agag came to him confidently, thinking, "Surely the bitterness of death is past." [33] But Samuel said, "As your sword has made women childless, so will your mother be childless among women." And Samuel put Agag to death before the LORD at Gilgal. [34] Then Samuel left for Ramah, but Saul went up to his home in Gibeah of Saul. [35] Until the day Samuel died, he did not go to see Saul again, though Samuel mourned for him. And the LORD was grieved that he had made Saul king over Israel.

## The Act of Disobedience (1 Samuel 15:1–9)

The people of Israel had judges who ruled over them for many years before they begged the prophet Samuel to ask God to give them a king. Samuel had tried to warn them that they would regret having a monarch, but they wanted to be like the other nations surrounding them. God directed Samuel to anoint Saul as Israel's first king. Although Saul enjoyed military successes, he proved to be arrogant and impulsive. He directly disobeyed God's instruction when he impatiently offered a sacrifice that he did not have the authority to make (1 Samuel 13). Sadly, this pattern continued.

The passage for today tells the story of how Saul sealed his destiny as a failed king. God gave Saul a message through Samuel that he was to lead his men to accomplish the fulfillment of a promise God had made back in the time of Moses (Exodus 17:15–16). The Amalekites were a people who had hindered the children of Israel during their wilderness wanderings and continued to harass the Israelites who lived near them.

Saul was given the assignment to completely wipe out the people, as God had promised.

In human terms, we may sometimes get uncomfortable with the idea that God ordered the death of men, women, and children. But we forget that God does not only see people in their current state; he sees their future too. Could there be any doubt that the youngest of the Amalekites, if they had been allowed to live, would have grown up to be a people who mocked God and attacked his followers? As hard as it may be to accept, death was a kinder outcome.

Not only were the people to be destroyed, but all their possessions as well. Soldiers customarily took plunder from the people they conquered as a reward for their service. If everything valuable was destroyed, they would not be tempted to fight for God for the wrong reasons.

Saul started out on the right foot. He mustered a sizeable army, came up with a plan, and warned the Kenites, who had been kind to the Israelites, to get out of the way (see Judges 1:16). Saul's army overpowered the Amalekites, and they accomplished what God had asked them to do—almost. Saul spared the Amalekite king Agag and the best of his livestock. Everything that was of inferior quality the soldiers were more than happy to destroy.

The temptation to save the best animals may be easy to understand, but why spare the enemy's king? Perhaps Saul felt sorry for a fellow leader; perhaps he saw the possibility of some monetary gain or some other strategic advantage. Maybe he enjoyed taunting and torturing his captive. At any rate, his obedience was not complete.

## The Futility of Disobedience (1 Samuel 15:10–23)

God spoke to Samuel again and gave him the bad news that Saul had disobeyed his direct command. The word translated "grieved" is the same word used in Genesis 6:7 when God was grieved over what the human race had become during the time of Noah. God had not changed his mind; he knew before he directed Samuel to anoint Saul as king that Saul would disobey him. But his knowledge of Saul's actions did not prevent God from feeling the pain of regret over Saul's disobedience.

Samuel was greatly distressed by this turn of events. He had invested time and effort in Saul and his success as king. The word translated "troubled" contains the idea of anger. The fact that Samuel had predicted that a king of Israel might not turn out to be what the people had hoped for did not make him feel any better.

Samuel did not delay confronting Saul. He got up early the next morning to find him. Ironically, Saul had set up a monument to himself and his great exploits before going to Gilgal, the place where he had last been chided by Samuel for offering an improper sacrifice. When Samuel found Saul, Saul opened the conversation by confidently offering his blessing on Samuel and bragging on his accomplishment of the task God had given him.

The evidence that Saul had disobeyed was painfully loud and clear: the animals that he had allowed to live were within earshot. Saul had a lot of explaining to do. But as he had done before (1 Sam. 13), he passed the blame to his soldiers. Notice Saul's use of pronouns in verse 15. "They" (the soldiers) spared the animals for sacrifice to "your" (Samuel's) God, but "we" (Saul and the soldiers) destroyed the rest. Saul took credit for what was commendable, but he tried to disown the responsibility for the animals that had been spared.

Samuel was in no mood to continue to listen to Saul's blame game, and he cut him off. He made it clear that he was bringing a message from God. Samuel reminded Saul that God had brought him out of obscurity to his place of leadership; Saul had done nothing to deserve the honor. And Samuel pointed out that the destruction of the Amalekites was not Saul's idea; it was *God's mission*. Therefore, Saul did not have the authority to carry out the task any way he wanted. He was bound to follow God's instructions to the letter. Samuel directly confronted Saul with his disobedience and the fact that he "pounced" (like a bird of prey) on the plunder when the opportunity presented itself. Samuel was not letting him get away with shifting blame; the word "you" appears seven times in verses 17–19.

Saul's reply showed his stubbornness: "But I did obey the Lord" (15:20). It is almost humorous the way he contradicted himself by claiming he "completely destroyed" the Amalekites at the same time he admitted he spared their king. Once again he blamed the soldiers for saving the best of the livestock for the purpose of sacrificing them to Samuel's God. It was almost as if Saul was using the argument that if God wanted all the animals destroyed, at least they could be a part of a ritual honoring God. (Incidentally, the meat could be shared among the men, which would

---

## NAHAM

*Naham* means "a change of heart or disposition, a change of mind, a change of purpose, or a change of one's conduct."[1] Sometimes the Bible describes God in terms of human emotions, such as anger, or in this case, regret. God is always consistent in his purposes. His character and his righteousness never change. His actions are not dependent on human activity. However, God can experience grief and sorrow over his people choosing to disobey him and knowing they will not turn back to him and must face the consequences of their sin.

---

have been a boost to Saul's popularity.) He was trying to make the case that ultimately he was following God's instructions, just doing it in a slightly different way. He attempted to make his motives sound so noble!

Samuel's answer in verses 22–23 is in poetic form. He made it clear that God is more interested in obedience than following a ritual, even one with good intentions. Disobedience is as bad in God's eyes as sorcery or idolatry. In either case, putting anything above God is sin. As a direct consequence of rejecting God's commands, Saul had been rejected as king.

## The Consequences of Disobedience (1 Samuel 15:24–35)

Belatedly, Saul admitted that he had sinned. Yet even then, Saul gave the excuse that he had given in to the people's wishes because he was afraid of them. Not taking responsibility for disobedience dates back to the garden of Eden. (Do you remember that Adam blamed Eve, and Eve blamed the serpent for disobeying God's command?) Saul seemed to want to have a "do over." He wanted everything to be forgiven and forgotten so things could go back to the way they were before his latest failure.

But Samuel made it clear that Saul had turned a corner in his position as God's leader. There was no going back at that point. In a desperate move, Saul grasped Samuel's robe as he turned to leave, tearing it in the

## DEVELOPING THE HABIT

Here are some ways to develop the habit of obedience in your life:

- Seek to come to a full understanding of what God is asking you to do.
- Refuse to be distracted by your own assessment of the way to accomplish God's purposes.
- Resist the temptation to form excuses for incomplete obedience.
- Be quick to confess to God when you have strayed from his direction.

process. Samuel used this as a teachable moment; he proclaimed that the kingdom had been "torn" from Saul (15:28). He re-emphasized that God does not change his mind about suffering the consequences of sin.

Once more Saul confessed and begged for Samuel's consideration. Now Saul's motives became clearer. It seems that his main concern was about his reputation in the eyes of the people. He wanted to keep up the appearance of God's favor whether it was real or not. Samuel finally agreed, but he had one last task to complete—a task that Saul should have taken care of himself. He called for Agag and put him to death, finally finishing the job Saul had started (15:32–33).

Verses 34–35 are a sad end to a sad story. The relationship between Samuel and Saul was forever severed. Both Samuel and God were grieving over the tragic turn of events.

## Implications and Actions

We often want to make excuses for our incomplete obedience to God's commands. We can be creative in our explanations of why we cannot accomplish what God has asked us to do or in our assignment of blame to others. But God is not fooled. He does not ask us to do anything that we are not capable of doing. We should not try to "second guess" God by coming up with our own way of fulfilling his commands. We simply need to obey, without questioning and without hesitation. Only then can we experience the blessings of being in the center of God's will.

## QUESTIONS

1. Have you ever been frustrated by a child who did the very least he or she could and failed to complete a task you had assigned? Can you imagine how God must feel when you treat him the same way?

2. List the excuses Saul gave for not obeying God completely.

3. In what ways have you tried to substitute your own methods for
   God's clear direction in the accomplishment of his will?

4. How can you ensure that you are obeying God completely?

## NOTES

1. Spiros Zodhiates and Warren Baker. *Hebrew-Greek Key Word Study Bible—New International Version,* (Chattanooga: TN: AMG Publishers, 1996), 1533.

# LESSON EIGHT
## *Prayer*

**FOCAL TEXTS**
Luke 11:1–13; 18:1–8

**BACKGROUND TEXT**
Luke 11:1–13; 18:1–8

**MAIN IDEA**
Disciples persistently offer faithful prayers to God.

**QUESTION TO EXPLORE**
Do I persistently offer faithful prayers to God?

**STUDY AIM**
To examine my time spent in prayer and to choose to persistently offer faithful prayers to God

**QUICK READ**
Jesus taught his disciples a model prayer which included worship, intercession, and petition. Jesus also emphasized the power of persistence in prayer to a loving God.

## Introduction

The surgeon Atul Gawande's book *The Checklist Manifesto* shows how doctors can use checklists to save lives and reduce mistakes, especially during surgery. Gawande's surgery checklist includes the following three "pause points": before anesthesia, before incision, and before leaving the operating room. Each pause point is designed to add a "speed bump" before an important task so people stop and think about what they are about to do. The results are striking.[1]

That's also a good idea for every follower of Christ. Developing pause points throughout the day and using those moments to pray could produce miraculous results.

# Luke 11:1–13

[1] One day Jesus was praying in a certain place. When he finished, one of his disciples said to him, "Lord, teach us to pray, just as John taught his disciples." [2] He said to them, "When you pray, say: "'Father, hallowed be your name, your kingdom come. [3] Give us each day our daily bread. [4] Forgive us our sins, for we also forgive everyone who sins against us. And lead us not into temptation.' " [5] Then he said to them, "Suppose one of you has a friend, and he goes to him at midnight and says, 'Friend, lend me three loaves of bread, [6] because a friend of mine on a journey has come to me, and I have nothing to set before him.' [7] "Then the one inside answers, 'Don't bother me. The door is already locked, and my children are with me in bed. I can't get up and give you anything.' [8] I tell you, though he will not get up and give him the bread because he is his friend, yet because of the man's boldness he will get up and give him as much as he needs. [9] "So I say to you: Ask and it will be given to you; seek and you will find; knock and the door will be opened to you. [10] For everyone who asks receives; he who seeks finds; and to him who knocks, the door will be opened. [11] "Which of you fathers, if your son asks for a fish, will give him a snake instead? [12] Or if he asks for an egg, will give him a scorpion? [13] If you then, though you are evil, know how to give

good gifts to your children, how much more will your Father in heaven give the Holy Spirit to those who ask him!"

# LUKE 18:1–8

¹ Then Jesus told his disciples a parable to show them that they should always pray and not give up. ² He said: "In a certain town there was a judge who neither feared God nor cared about men. ³ And there was a widow in that town who kept coming to him with the plea, 'Grant me justice against my adversary.' ⁴ "For some time he refused. But finally he said to himself, 'Even though I don't fear God or care about men, ⁵ yet because this widow keeps bothering me, I will see that she gets justice, so that she won't eventually wear me out with her coming!'" ⁶ And the Lord said, "Listen to what the unjust judge says. ⁷ And will not God bring about justice for his chosen ones, who cry out to him day and night? Will he keep putting them off ? ⁸ I tell you, he will see that they get justice, and quickly. However, when the Son of Man comes, will he find faith on the earth?"

## Jesus Teaches on Prayer (11:1–13)

Some question whether the prayer Jesus taught was meant to be recited, or studied as a pattern for all prayer. Certainly, one could answer in the affirmative on both counts. There is nothing wrong with reciting the prayer verbatim as a regular practice. However, there is also much to be gained by studying Jesus' prayer, and using it as a template for our prayer life.

Luke 11:1–13 can be divided into four parts: (1) the request of the disciples; (2) the Model Prayer; (3) a parable calling for persistence in prayer; and (4) a parable affirming the loving generosity of God.

## The Request of the Disciples (11:1)

The disciples asked Jesus to teach them to pray, just as John the Baptist had taught his disciples. Jesus had been baptized by John, and for a brief period of time the two had a parallel ministry in the southern region of the Jordan River valley. After John was imprisoned by Herod Antipas, Jesus moved his ministry to the northwest region of the Sea of Galilee. Several of Jesus' disciples had previously been disciples of John the Baptist (John 1:35–42). They had learned a certain pattern of prayer in their time with John.

The disciples didn't need Jesus to teach them how to pray, in general. However, they had noticed that prayer was one of Jesus' most consistent habits (Luke 3:21; 5:16; 6:12; 9:18, 28–29; 18:1; 22:41, 44). One day, after watching Jesus pray, they asked him to teach them how to pattern their prayers after his. Their desire was to experience the power and effectiveness of Jesus' prayers.

## The Model Prayer (11:2–4)

Jesus' prayer began with a focus on God, moved to the needs of others, and culminated with the concerns of the one who was praying. In other words, it began with praise, moved to intercession, and concluded with petition.

The opening lines of the prayer offer a glimpse into the intimate nature of Jesus' prayer life. He called God, "Father." This was a term most often used of God in combination with other words (i.e., heavenly, God, holy, etc.) and emphasized the majesty, glory, and holiness of God. The Greek word for Father used in this verse (*pater*), could be associated with the Aramaic personal word for Father, "Abba." Elsewhere, Paul advocated the usage of "Abba", in reference to prayer (Galatians 4:6). This was the equivalent of calling God, "Daddy."

In praising the Father, Jesus called for his name to be hallowed (regarded as holy) and for his kingdom to come. Matthew added the words, "on earth as it is in heaven" (Matthew 6:10). Jesus was calling for God to act in powerful and visible ways upon the earth. Even as we praise God who is in heaven, we are calling on him to make his name known throughout the earth, and foreshadowing the day when "every knee should bow, in heaven and on earth and under the earth, and every tongue confess that Jesus Christ is Lord, to the glory of God the Father" (Philippians 2:10–11).

Jesus' prayer quickly moved from praise to intercession. The request for bread reflected the general concern for the needs of the world. Bread was considered to be the basic element for the sustenance of the body. It often represented all food, and was sometimes used as a metaphor for God's provision (John 6:48). The request for daily *bread* echoed the wilderness experience of the Hebrew people, where God provided manna and quail on a daily basis (Numbers 11:7–9). The fact that Jesus asked for *daily* bread, reflected a desire to have only what was necessary, and no more. An excess of material wealth can have a negative effect on one's ability to trust God (Matthew 19:23–24).

Finally, Jesus concluded his prayer with a two-fold petition: (1) the forgiveness of sins; and (2) the avoidance of temptation. After interceding on behalf of the entire world, Jesus called his disciples to pray for their own spiritual lives. We will not be able to help the world for long if we are crippled by our own sin. When Paul instructed the leaders at Ephesus to care for the church, he first commanded them to take care of their own spiritual health (Acts 20:28).

## A Parable on Persistent Prayer (11:5–10)

After offering the prayer, Jesus told a parable. The parable was designed to encourage the disciples to be persistent and faithful in their prayer lives. In the parable Jesus painted a familiar picture for his listeners. Village life was built upon the principle of a shared existence.

The people of first century Palestine lived in an agricultural society under oppressive rule. They were forced to unite their resources into small tribal communities in order to survive. This process of survival was also facilitated by the ancient Hebrew cultural imperative of hospitality. In ancient times, the responsibility to care for a neighbor, friend, or even a stranger was written into the moral fabric of the community (Genesis18; Exodus 22:21; Leviticus 19:10, 34, 25:35).

Jesus' parable reflected both the social pressure to share and the human reality that sharing was never easy on the one making the sacrifice. In the parable, a man comes to his neighbor in the middle of the night asking for hospitality. The neighbor is naturally annoyed because of the inconvenience. The parable seemed to indicate that the man had the means to comply with the request, but was reluctant to make the necessary sacrifice. It was only because the man in need persisted, that the neighbor eventually rose to grant the request for hospitality.

This parable offered a contrast. Although the neighbor was reluctant to offer hospitality, he did so based solely on the man's bold and persistent asking. Jesus then emphasized that such persistence in prayer pays off.

Luke 11:9–10 are two of the most misunderstood verses in the Bible. The point of the parable has nothing to do with the content of our prayers. Jesus was speaking specifically about the commitment to prayer and persistence in prayer. The focus was on *bold asking,* not on what we are to ask for.

The content of prayer was covered in the model prayer (11:3–4). Jesus instructed us to ask for God's will to be done on earth, that our minimal needs be met (daily bread), and that he protect our spiritual lives from sin and temptation. In other words, there was no promise in this passage that God would give us whatever we may want from our selfish wish list. On the contrary, if we pray selflessly (as modeled in Jesus' prayer), and persistently, God will answer our prayers. The joyful point of Jesus' parable is that we have the certainty of God's response to bold and persistent prayer.

## A Parable of a Loving God (11:11–13)

Jesus ended this teaching with another parable. This story, like the one before it, was told to contrast the frail and imperfect nature of human love as compared to the perfect love of God. The parable came in the form of a question. If a man's son asks for a fish, the father will not give him a snake, will he? (11:11). The obvious answer is "no." If a fallible human father knows how to love his child, how much more will a perfect heavenly father know how to love his own?

## The Persistent Widow (18:1–8)

Jesus told another parable that reinforced this teaching. Jesus and his disciples had been discussing the coming of the kingdom of God. As the disciples awaited his return, he encouraged them to pray constantly, especially in difficult times (Luke 18:1).

In a certain village there was a judge who didn't care what anyone thought, including God. There was also a poor widow who had a case

## DEAR ABBA

According to biblical scholar Joachim Jeremias, the Aramaic term, "Abba", was behind Jesus' usage of the word "Father." Jeremias examined the immense and rich prayer literature of late Judaism, and was unable to find a single instance of God being addressed as "Abba."[2] Add to that the fact that God was seldom referred to as "Father" in the Old Testament and the inevitable conclusion is that Jesus was introducing something new. "Abba" was the most intimate form of the word "Father." It was patterned after the first sounds that a child stammers.

Jesus, unlike his contemporaries or those who came before him, was so bold as to talk to God in the intimate, guttural language of a small child, just learning to speak. The most astounding thing is that he encouraged his disciples to approach God in the same, intimate way. The nervousness with which the early Christians approached the opening to the prayer is evident in the so-called St. John Chrysostom preface to the Lord's Prayer: "And make us worthy O Lord, that we may joyously, and without presumption may make bold to invoke Thee, the heavenly God, as Father, and to say: Our Father."[3]

before the judge. She pleaded with the judge for justice, but he refused. The judge was one of many magistrates who worked for the Roman legal system. His aim was not to find justice, but rather to keep the peace. He did not care about God or the people because his allegiance was to Rome.

PAX ROMANA or "Roman Peace" was maintained through a network of terror. As such, the judge would not have cared one bit about justice for the woman; only that she not cause a stir. The woman, of course, as a female and a widow, would have been one of the most vulnerable and powerless of the society. The vulnerability and poverty of widows and orphans is almost a truism of the Bible (Exodus 22:22–24; Isaiah 1:17; 1 Timothy 5:3; James 1:27).

The powerless widow brilliantly used her only available leverage: persistence. Finally, just to get rid of her, the unsympathetic judge decided to give the woman what she wanted. The phrase "wear me out" (Luke 18:5) means "give a black eye to." The unjust judge finally acted because

## Practicing Prayer

- Pray a one-minute-prayer, every sixty minutes throughout a single day.
- Memorize the Lord's Prayer and pray it three times a day.
- Practice patterning your daily prayers after the Model Prayer. Begin with a time of praising and thanking God. Bring requests to God on behalf of others. Ask God to help you in your own spiritual life. Try doing this every day for a week.

he was concerned about possible damage to his reputation with Rome. She was becoming such a pest that he was afraid of the only thing that could hurt him with Rome—a riot or revolt. In the end, it was her relentless and dogged petitioning that brought justice.

Jesus then made the application. If this heartless judge would finally do the right thing for the wrong reasons, how much more likely is it that our perfect Judge in heaven will do the right thing, and for all the right reasons! Once again, Jesus revealed his heavenly Father to be a loving, kind, and just God.

## Implications and Actions

Jesus showed his disciples how to pray and encouraged them to be bold and persistent in their prayers. Christians should worship God through prayer on a daily basis. Jesus also called on his disciples to intercede for others in prayer, and to ask for help with their own spiritual needs. Christians should faithfully intercede for others and focus daily on their own spiritual growth. When we model our prayers after those of Jesus we experience the power of God in our lives. In prayer we discover that we have a loving and caring God who is pleased to answer our prayers.

## QUESTIONS

1. What is the longest you have prayed for something before God answered? How did it feel to wait?

2. What is your most persistent prayer? What have you learned from it?

3. How do you think prayer helps you? How does it change you?

4.  What do you do when God doesn't answer your prayer?

5.  If God is loving and caring, why does he seem to answer some prayers and not answer others?

NOTES ──────────────────────────────────────────────

1.  Frank Partnoy, *Wait: The Art and Science of Delay* (New York: Public Affairs, 2012), 181–183.

2.  Joachim Jeremias, *Jesus and the Message of the New Testament* (Minneapolis, Minnesota: Fortress Press, 2002), 50–51.

3.  Ibid., 52.

# LESSON NINE
## *Purity*

### FOCAL TEXTS
Psalm 24:1–6; Ephesians 5:1–16

### BACKGROUND
Psalm 24:1–6; Ephesians 5:1–16

### MAIN IDEA
Disciples pursue a life of purity.

### QUESTION TO EXPLORE
How can I pursue purity
in an impure world?

### STUDY AIM
To choose to pursue purity
in my thoughts, attitudes,
words, and actions

### QUICK READ
God calls his followers to
live pure lives in the midst of
an impure world. Doing so
results in authentic worship
that reflects Christ to all.

## Introduction

The cable television show, *Hoarders,* chronicles the trials and tribulations of people who can't throw anything away. One apartment manager had a couple whom she had to evict. They were living in total squalor. She had warned them in writing about their behavior. Finally, after months of pleading, she had to forcefully evict them. Why? During their entire time in the apartment, almost a year, they hadn't once taken out the trash. The property management company needed to bring in a forty-foot dumpster just to clean out the apartment!

If we are not watchful, filth can fill our lives. In fact, slavery to sin doesn't occur overnight. It is a process of hoarding evil thoughts, attitudes, and actions over a long period of time. The Bible's call to purity is the antidote to a life of suffocating sin.

# PSALM 24:1–6

[1] The earth is the LORD's, and everything in it, the world, and all who live in it; [2] for he founded it upon the seas and established it upon the waters. [3] Who may ascend the hill of the LORD? Who may stand in his holy place? [4] He who has clean hands and a pure heart, who does not lift up his soul to an idol or swear by what is false. [5] He will receive blessing from the LORD and vindication from God his Savior. [6] Such is the generation of those who seek him, who seek your face, O God of Jacob.

# EPHESIANS 5:1–16

[1] Be imitators of God, therefore, as dearly loved children [2] and live a life of love, just as Christ loved us and gave himself up for us as a fragrant offering and sacrifice to God. [3] But among you there must not be even a hint of sexual immorality, or of any kind of impurity, or of greed, because these are improper for God's holy people. [4] Nor should there be obscenity, foolish talk or coarse joking, which are out of place, but rather thanksgiving. [5] For of this you can be sure: No immoral, impure or greedy person—such a man is an idolater—has any inheritance in the kingdom of

Christ and of God. <sup>6</sup> Let no one deceive you with empty words, for because of such things God's wrath comes on those who are disobedient. <sup>7</sup> Therefore do not be partners with them. <sup>8</sup> For you were once darkness, but now you are light in the Lord. Live as children of light <sup>9</sup> (for the fruit of the light consists in all goodness, righteousness and truth) <sup>10</sup> and find out what pleases the Lord. <sup>11</sup> Have nothing to do with the fruitless deeds of darkness, but rather expose them. <sup>12</sup> For it is shameful even to mention what the disobedient do in secret. <sup>13</sup> But everything exposed by the light becomes visible, <sup>14</sup> for it is light that makes everything visible. This is why it is said: "Wake up, O sleeper, rise from the dead, and Christ will shine on you." <sup>15</sup> Be very careful, then, how you live—not as unwise but as wise, <sup>16</sup> making the most of every opportunity, because the days are evil.

## Pure Worship (Psalm 24:1–6)

There is an interesting connection between Psalms 22, 23, and 24. Psalm 22 paints a portrait of the sacrificial God who is willing to give himself for his creation. Psalm 23 introduces the caring God who gently shepherds his creation from beginning to end. And finally, Psalm 24 sings of the omnipotent, sovereign God who is king over all he created. Psalm 24 concludes with worship as the appropriate response to the God who is not only sacrificial and caring, but who is also the omnipotent creator of all things.

Psalm 24:1–6 can be divided into two parts: (1) a description of God as creator (v.1–2); and (2) the purity requirements for approaching God in worship (v.3–6).

## God as Creator (24:1–2)

The psalmist established God as the creator of all things. He used the word for "earth" to proclaim that God created everything that exists on earth. He used the word for "world" to emphasize that God also created everything beyond the earth. The psalmist had an understanding of the creation account in Genesis, as is evident from his reference to the waters and seas. This came from the ancient belief that before God began his creative process, the earth was covered with water (Genesis 1:2). The critical point was that God was present before creation came into existence.

## Requirements for Worship (24:3–6)

Since God desires worship, every person should prepare themselves to worship God. The psalmist made his point by asking a question and then answering it. The two rhetorical questions cut to the heart of worship (24:3). We are not worthy to stand in his presence because God is holy, omnipotent, omniscient, and omnipresent, and we are not. The first question, "Who may ascend the hill of the Lord?" referred to Mt. Zion in Jerusalem where the temple stood. It was considered the most holy spot on the face of the earth. It was considered the navel of the earth, and the place where God spoke. This psalm was most likely sung by pilgrims as they made their way to Jerusalem for one of the annual festivals.

The second question, "Who may stand in his holy place?" referred to the temple itself. The temple was off limits to those who were unclean or those outside of the covenant with God. There were purification requirements and rituals that had to be observed in order to enter the temple. The steps leading up to the temple mount were lined with water cisterns in which the pilgrims could find purification. Any sacrifice offered at the temple had to be pre-approved by the priests on duty. If there was any blemish or defect found, the sacrificial animal would be rejected.

By the first century there was a system in place for the benefit of pilgrims who had traveled from afar. Animals pre-approved for sacrifice could be purchased in an area adjacent to the temple. All of this was in place to assure the purity of all those who entered the temple, as well as the sacrifices offered there.

The psalmist answered the requirement question by describing the worshippers who met the qualifications for purity. They had "clean hands and a pure heart" (24:4). Hands were most often used as a metaphor for action. Clean hands, therefore, were a metaphor for right actions. Right actions were always linked to adherence to the Mosaic Law. The first requirement for entrance into the presence of God, therefore, was ethical purity according to the Law. The second followed closely: purity of motive. The psalmist called for a pure heart. The heart was considered the source of volition. Following the Mosaic Law was important. However, following the letter of the law was insufficient, if the motives were wrong. A pure heart signaled an ethical life established on the motive of absolute love of God.

The concept of clean hands and a pure heart was amplified in Psalm 15, also a "song of David." Psalm 15 began in a similar fashion to Psalm 24, with a series of two questions related to who was worthy to ascend Mount Zion, and enter the sacred temple. Also like Psalm 24, Psalm 15 addressed the ethical behavior and motivation of the worshipper. The worshipper who was worthy to stand in the presence of God was blameless, righteous, and always truthful from the heart. This person treated others with honor and respect. Most of the psalm referenced the worshipper's action toward others. It affirmed the psalmist's emphasis on the inherent connection between love of God and love of neighbor.

The reward for seeking God with a pure heart and clean hands was God's blessing and vindication (24:5). The worshippers enjoyed the fulfillment of his promises, which included provision and protection. These benefits were enjoyed by a generation that sought a personal relationship with God, rather than following rules to avoid punishment (Ps. 24:6).

## Pure Living in an Impure World (Ephesians 5:1–16)

The Apostle Paul picked up on this theme in his letter to the Ephesians. The city of Ephesus was the center of worship of the goddess Artemis. The temple built for the worship of Artemis was considered one of the Seven Wonders of the Ancient World. It was an important part of the Ephesian economy, and a cultural fixture.

As Paul attempted to strengthen the Christian church at Ephesus he was concerned about the strong pagan influence in Ephesian society, and the syncretism that was common in the Greek world (1 Timothy 1:3–4). He was afraid that some of the Christians were incorporating cultural traditions associated with the worship of Artemis into Christian worship. He called the Christians to set themselves apart from the pagan culture that surrounded them so they could approach God free from the idolatry that plagued so many other belief systems (1 Tim. 4:1–5; Ephesians 4:17). Paul called them to maintain pure hearts and clean lives (Eph. 5:8–12).

His call to do so in Ephesians 5:1–14 was set in the larger context of calling Christians to a new life in Christ. Paul exhorted them to be prisoners for the Lord, humbling themselves in service and love for each other (4:1–2). He encouraged them to rise up in the calling God had placed on their lives (4:7–13). He called them to live in a way different from the pagan culture around them (4:17). He also called them to completely abandon their former way of life in order to embrace the way of Christ (4:20–24).

Paul detailed the specific things that differentiated Christians from all others, and called them to embrace these differences (4:31). Finally, and above all else, he called on the Christians to love and forgive one another, pointing to Christ as the ultimate example of forgiving love (4:32).

Paul moved from general to specific examples of how Christians could make conscious choices regarding their attitudes and actions. He lifted up Jesus as the supreme example of sacrificial love (5:1). In moving to the more specific, Paul outlined several areas of particular concern with respect to purity. Paul addressed sexual immorality, greed, and sins of speech. He combined these together and considered all of them forms of idolatry based on self-indulgence (5:5).

Sexual immorality for instance, is a persistent temptation in our self-consumed culture. Movies, television programs, magazines, the Internet, and many forms of social media offer the temptation of sexual immorality. It is one of the most pervasive forms of sin in our world today and is always based on a desire to please self.

Greed is another prevalent sin. Greed is the desire to consume more and more, even though I already have plenty. Greed never considers the other person, but rather is always concerned with self. The insatiable desire for more money, sex, possessions, or attention is not proper for God's people who have been called to holiness.

Paul also mentioned abusive speech as a particularly pernicious sin. Our speech reflects the condition of our hearts (Matthew 12:34, James 3:1–12). Paul proclaimed that Christians are called to purity, not only in how they talk, but also in what they talk about. There is no room for obscene stories, foolish talk, or coarse jokes (Ephesians 5:4). This type of speech is also self-indulgent and hurtful to others.

## THE TEMPLE OF ARTEMIS

The Temple of Artemis, located in Ephesus, was a little larger than a football field and was built of marble, Cyprus wood paneling, and cedar roof beams. It was the largest building known in antiquity and was considered one of the Seven Wonders of the World.

The goddess Artemis went through many transformations throughout the centuries. Numerous statues representing her image have been found. Typically, the lower half of her body depicts an animal and the upper half a female human being. Often she is many-breasted, most likely portraying her fertility and her role as the nourisher of Ephesian culture. There were two annual festivals in honor of Artemis, which included religious processions as well as athletic and theatrical competitions. For centuries much of life in Ephesus revolved around the temple of Artemis.

There is no consensus on what the worship of Artemis included. However, Ephesus was always closely associated with the practice of magic. This is confirmed by Luke's account of the challenges Paul faced while preaching there (Acts 19:19).

Paul called all of these things idolatry. This was the most serious indictment anyone could offer. Idolatry was defined in the Mosaic Law as placing anything before God (Exodus 20:3–4). It is possible for us to minimize sin and excuse it, especially when we believe that no one else is being hurt by it. But here, Paul indicated that God is the one who is offended by our sin because in our self-indulgence we have placed ourselves above God. In light of this connection to idolatry, it is difficult to minimize sin, and a mistake to follow those who would live in such a manner (Ephesians 5:5–7).

Finally, Paul drew a contrast between those who live in the light and those who dwell in darkness. He encouraged Christians to avoid all involvement with evildoers (5:7). Although at one time evildoers themselves, the Christians had been changed by the power of God (5:8a). For this reason Paul admonished them to walk as children of light (5:8b–10).

Paul then detailed, more specifically, the characteristics of those who walk in the light. Those who walk in the light of Christ will produce the fruit of the Spirit which is goodness, righteousness, and truth (Galatians

## Pathways to Purity

- Try a technology fast. See how long you can go without watching television or videos, or accessing the Internet.
- Renew your commitment of absolute fidelity to your spouse. Seal your commitment with a meaningful ceremony, including a signed certificate.
- Talk to your children about keeping themselves pure (in body, mind, and spirit.)
- Watch the movie, *A Walk to Remember* with your older children, and discuss the values demonstrated by the lead female character.

5:22–23). He reminded them that these things are pleasing to God (Ephesians 5:10). He commanded them to expose the evildoers because their works are shameful (5:11–12). In the end, the light of God will show the true character of a person's works (5:13).

## Implications and Actions

The psalmist calls us to worship a holy and majestic Creator. In order to do this we must have pure motives and attitudes (a pure heart), as well as right living (clean hands). Paul also called the Christians at Ephesus to live their lives with purity of thoughts, attitudes, and actions. This means that Christians should live in stark contrast to the culture around them. People should be able to see a difference in the way a Christian lives in comparison to the morals and values of the world. Christians should seek to love all people, but not imitate the sinful lifestyle of others. Christians should also deal honestly with their own sin, bringing it into the light of Jesus where he can forgive and heal all things.

## QUESTIONS

1.  What are some things you can do to protect yourself from impure thoughts and actions?

2.  What are some sources of temptation that could lead you to impure thoughts or actions?

3.  What can you do to prepare yourself for worship?

4.  What are some excuses you make for the sin in your life?

5.  What does purity look like in the 21st Century? Has it changed from previous eras?

# LESSON TEN
## *Service*

**FOCAL TEXTS**
Mark 10:35–45; John
13:12–17; James 2:14–17

**BACKGROUND**
Mark 10:35–45; John
13:12–17; James 2:14–17

**MAIN IDEA**
Disciples follow Jesus'
example of serving others.

**QUESTION TO EXPLORE**
How am I following Jesus'
example of serving others?

**STUDY AIM**
To decide how I will follow
Jesus' example by serving
someone in the coming week

**QUICK READ**
Jesus taught his disciples that
being a servant was the most
important thing any Christian
could do. Jesus modeled
sacrificial service and calls
us to follow his example.

## Introduction

While preparing a sermon, a pastor posted this question to his friends on Facebook: "What makes it hard for you to serve other people?" They gave some great answers, including:

- "Serving is hard when it doesn't fit into my schedule or plan. Like when I want to go for a walk or take a long bath, but my aging parent needs me to sort their meds, run an errand, or simply be with them."
- "It's hard when their needs seem endless. I don't want to risk helping/serving because I may get sucked in."

But my favorite answer was this one: "What makes it hard to serve others? Others!"

It is easy to make excuses for failing to serve others. However, serving others is not an elective for the Christian. It is a required course.

# MARK 10:35–45

[35] Then James and John, the sons of Zebedee, came to him. "Teacher," they said, "we want you to do for us whatever we ask." [36] "What do you want me to do for you?" he asked. [37] They replied, "Let one of us sit at your right and the other at your left in your glory." [38] "You don't know what you are asking," Jesus said. "Can you drink the cup I drink or be baptized with the baptism I am baptized with?" [39] "We can," they answered. Jesus said to them, "You will drink the cup I drink and be baptized with the baptism I am baptized with, [40] but to sit at my right or left is not for me to grant. These places belong to those for whom they have been prepared." [41] When the ten heard about this, they became indignant with James and John. [42] Jesus called them together and said, "You know that those who are regarded as rulers of the Gentiles lord it over them, and their high officials exercise authority over them. [43] Not so with you. Instead, whoever wants to become great among you must be your servant, [44] and whoever wants to be first must be slave of all. [45] For even the Son of Man

did not come to be served, but to serve, and to give his life as a ransom for many."

# JOHN 13:12–17

12 When he had finished washing their feet, he put on his clothes and returned to his place. "Do you understand what I have done for you?" he asked them. 13 "You call me 'Teacher' and 'Lord,' and rightly so, for that is what I am.14 Now that I, your Lord and Teacher, have washed your feet, you also should wash one another's feet. 15 I have set you an example that you should do as I have done for you. 16 I tell you the truth, no servant is greater than his master, nor is a messenger greater than the one who sent him. 17 Now that you know these things, you will be blessed if you do them.

# JAMES 2:14–17

14 What good is it, my brothers, if a man claims to have faith but has no deeds? Can such faith save him? 15 Suppose a brother or sister is without clothes and daily food. 16 If one of you says to him, "Go, I wish you well; keep warm and well fed," but does nothing about his physical needs, what good is it? 17 In the same way, faith by itself, if it is not accompanied by action, is dead.

## Greatness = Service (Mark 10:35–45)

The two brothers, James and John, approached Jesus with a request. This was a rather bold move. Not wanting to risk rejection, they first asked Jesus to fulfill whatever request they made. This amounted to asking for a blank check. It may have come as a reaction to what Jesus had been teaching about asking (Mark 11:24). They invoked the name of their master, Jesus, and expected him to answer in the affirmative, no matter the nature of their request.

James and John asked to sit on the right and left side of Jesus when he came into his kingdom. The two most important seats, after the throne of the king, were the seats to the right and left of the throne. This was a request for political power, and revealed a basic misunderstanding of Jesus' teaching.

James and John approached Jesus from a place of humility. They recognized that he was the rabbi who had the power to give them what they wanted. They also realized that as his disciples, they were only in a position to receive. However, their request would have reversed those roles. If Jesus had agreed to their original request, the disciples would have been in the position of power over Jesus because he would have been obligated to unconditionally submit to their request. Jesus didn't fall into that trap. This was made clear in the end, when he refused to grant their request.

This scene followed on the heels of Jesus' third and final prediction of his death. After each prediction Jesus described the type of service that would be required of his followers (Mark 8:31/8:34–9:1; 9:31/9:33–37; 10:32–34/10:38–45).

After his first prediction (Mark 8:31) Peter pulled Jesus aside and rebuked him. Jesus rebuked Peter, and then instructed the disciples on the proper role of the disciple of Jesus: a role of selfless and sacrificial service. The second prediction (Mark 9:31) basically repeated the lesson of the first. The disciples were arguing over who would be the greatest among them. Jesus corrected them by informing them that in the new kingdom, "if anyone wants to be first, he must be the very last, and the servant of all" (Mark 9:35).

The third and final scene affirmed the basic message of the first two. This time the lessons of humility and a life of service were found in Jesus' reaction to the request of James and John. Their request to sit on the right and left side of Jesus revealed the nature of the kingdom they had in mind. Mark reported that they simply did not understand what Jesus was trying to say, but were afraid to ask (Mark 9:32). There are two possible explanations as to why they, along with the other disciples, did not understand what seemed to be the plain teaching of Jesus concerning his impending death and resurrection.

The first was that they thought Jesus was teaching in parables. Jesus used parables in most of his teaching (Mark 4:33–34). It was possible that the disciples didn't know how to interpret Jesus' words on this teaching. Peter, obviously, took them literally in the first prediction. But in the second and third predictions it is unclear whether they understood the teaching to be literal or metaphorical.

## JESUS AND A POLITICAL REVOLUTION

There were many in first century Palestine who were hoping for a Messiah to lead them in a revolt against the Roman Empire. The Romans had controlled Palestine since 68 B.C., when the Roman general Pompey conquered the area. Client kings, loyal to Rome, had been selected to rule over the people. Herod was an example of this system of rule.

There had been several attempts to gain independence from Rome by force, but none of them succeeded. The words and actions of some of the disciples indicates that they may have perceived Jesus to be a Messiah who would lead a successful war of independence against Rome (Mark 8:31–33; John 11:16; 18:10–11). The war finally materialized in 66 A.D. and the Israelites were utterly defeated in 70 A.D. with the fall of Jerusalem. Jesus did not come to lead a military campaign against Rome. In the end, he was right: "for all who draw the sword will die by the sword" (Matthew 26:52).

If James and John were viewing Jesus' words symbolically, it would seem that they were asking to sit on the right and left hand of Jesus whenever he came into his kingdom, no matter when, where, or what that kingdom looked like. Their words may have been metaphorical to match his metaphorical teaching. Nonetheless, they were certainly asking to hold positions of penultimate power in the kingdom that was to come.

The second possibility was that James and John took Jesus' prediction literally. There was certainly some reason to believe that at least some of the disciples understood Jesus to mean that he was literally going to die in Jerusalem. When Jesus was summoned to Bethany because Lazarus was deathly ill, Jesus made the decision to go. The disciples had been with Jesus hiding in the wilderness of Judea because of an attempt to kill Jesus (John 11:8). Upon hearing that Jesus was traveling to Bethany, Thomas made the brave and predictive statement, "Let us also go, that we may die with him" (John 11:16).

It is possible that James and John believed Jesus was going to die in a great battle against the Roman power system. If that was the case, their request suggests that they were offering a succession plan, and were

---

### Case Study

One of the members of your Bible fellowship confides in you about some trouble she is having in her marriage. A lot of the trouble has to do with financial struggles. She asks you for prayer. You feel the Spirit calling you to do more. What can you do? How do you go about it? Who do you talk to? What is the best way to serve her and her family?

---

"sacrificially" volunteering to take over after Jesus was gone! James and John, together with Peter formed the most intimate, inner circle of Jesus' ministry. The fact that they, along with all the other disciples (as seen in the second prediction narrative) were expecting an earthly kingdom reveals the pervasive nature of the disciples' misunderstanding.

Jesus asked James and John if they were willing to pay the price that their request demanded. He used the metaphorical language of drinking from a cup. The cup was the cup of suffering. Jesus referred to this cup in the Garden of Gethsemane the night before his death (Mark 14:36). The cup, for Jesus, was sacrificial death. The brothers affirmed that they were ready to pay the price. Jesus informed them that they would indeed, some day, pay the price. But the positions of power in his kingdom were not his to give, but rather were for those "for whom they had been pre-pared" (Mark 10:40).

When the other disciples heard about the brothers' request, they were furious. This sort of infighting, jockeying for position, and petty jeal-ousy seemed to be common within the small group of disciples. They obviously felt that there was a lot to be gained by being close to Jesus. Jesus reminded them, once again, of the order of power within his king-dom. It is the servant who holds the most power. Jesus even pointed to himself as an example of one who "did not come to be served, but to serve, and to give his life as a ransom for many" (Mark 10:45). Here again, Jesus made an allusion to his impending death, and pointed to it as an example of sacrificial service.

The word "ransom" means the price paid for redeeming property, especially in the case of paying for slaves or captives. This is one of the most remarkable statements that Jesus made in this section of Scripture.

It seems to have as its foundation Isaiah 52:13—53:12, known as the Suffering Servant Song. There are several places in the song that indicate the idea of one who was sent to suffer and die in order to redeem the people (Isa. 53:5, 8, 11, 12).

Jesus modeled this command of sacrificial service, not only in the way he died for our sins, but also in the way he lived. This was not just a call to die to self, but also to live in such a way that the suffering service of Christ would be revealed. Jesus modeled this concept when he washed the feet of his disciples.

## An Example to Follow (John 13:12–17)

The night before his sacrificial death, Jesus observed the Passover meal with his disciples. The Passover meal was a remembrance of God's saving power in Egypt. Jesus gave it new meaning when he compared the bread and wine to his body and blood, respectively. He set the meal as a remembrance of his sacrificial act on the cross. After the meal he presented a living illustration of what it meant to be his disciple. Over their objections, Jesus took a basin of water and a towel, and performed the duty reserved for only the lowliest of slaves. He washed the feet of his disciples.

John focused on the theological meaning of the foot washing. Jesus was proclaiming that his disciples were clean (John 13:10). However, as he began to debrief his disciples on the experience he pointed to the practical application of what they had learned (13:12). If their "Teacher," and "Lord," had lowered himself to washing their feet, then they should have no hesitation in doing the same for each other. Jesus reminded them that the goal of a disciple is to be like his or her teacher (13:13–15). Therefore, they should follow his example and wash the feet of others (13:17).

## Faith in Action (James 2:14–17)

Jesus' call for his disciples to live out their faith is affirmed in the letter of James. James drew a close connection between faith and action when he wrote, "What good is it, my brothers, if someone claims to have faith but has no deeds? Can such faith save him?" (James 2:14). The answer to James' rhetorical question is "no." Such faith is insufficient, not because works produce salvation, but because a proclamation of faith, without a practical manifestation of it, rings hollow.

Talk is cheap, would be the essence of James' point. James was not advocating for people to seek to earn their salvation by works, but rather that Christian action is the evidence of true faith. In fact, James believed that faith and works were two sides of the same coin. That coin was what Jesus called the summation of the law: Love God and love each other (Mark 12:28–31).

After Jesus washed the feet of his disciples he commanded them to do the same and said, "By this all men will know that you are my disciples, if you love one another" (John 13:35). James confirmed this concept and added that the only way people can know that you love them is if you show it. That's why he writes, "faith by itself, if it is not accompanied by action, is dead" (James 2:17).


## Implications and Actions

When two of Jesus' disciples requested a position of power in his kingdom, he used the opportunity to teach them the centrality of service in the kingdom of God. We are called to place the needs of others above our own. We are called to reach out to others and minister to their needs. Jesus modeled this concept by washing the feet of his disciples.

Disciples of Jesus should be prepared to fulfill even the lowliest of tasks. We should always be aware of ways in which we can serve, no matter how simple or menial the task. In addition, James reminded the church that faith without works is useless. Disciples of Jesus demonstrate their faith in their daily interactions with others. We should seek ways to put our faith into action.

Ultimately, disciples of Jesus are called to make a difference in the world through sacrificial service and strategic action. The church that follows Jesus will make an impact in its community through faithful service to others.

## QUESTIONS

1. What are some of the ways you can serve people outside of your immediate family?

2. What would be the equivalent of washing someone's feet in the 21st Century?

3. What are some ways that you can put others first?

4. What are some things your church could do to serve its community?

5. What are some ways you could express your faith in action?

FOCAL TEXTS
Deuteronomy 8:10–18;
Matthew 25:14–30

BACKGROUND
Deuteronomy 8:1–20;
Matthew 25:1–46

MAIN IDEA
Disciples are faithful
stewards of all God has
entrusted to them.

QUESTION TO EXPLORE
Am I a faithful steward of all
God has entrusted to me?

STUDY AIM
To evaluate and increase the
faithfulness of my stewardship
of all God has entrusted to me

QUICK READ
Everything has been
given to us by God as a
stewardship. Someday it
will be returned to him, and
we will be held accountable
for what we did with it.

# LESSON ELEVEN
## *Stewardship*

## Introduction

Does money really buy happiness? Studies by a generation of behavioral scientists show that material goods usually don't deliver lasting happiness. But there is one way that money can buy happiness—when you spend money with and for others. Researchers call this phenomenon a "buying experience."

Elizabeth Dunn and Michael Norton, a pair of researchers who authored the book *Happy Money*, reported on the following experiment:

> We handed out Starbucks gift cards on a university campus
> . . . [and] told some people to head to Starbucks and buy some-
> thing for themselves. We told others to pass their gift card
> along to someone else. And we told a third group of people to
> use the gift card to buy something for someone else—with the
> additional requirement that they actually hang out with that
> person at Starbucks.[1]

Dunn and Norton concluded, "Who was happiest? Those who treated someone else and shared in that experience with them." These results should not be shocking to followers of Jesus. This is because God gives us everything we have so that we can share it with others.

## DEUTERONOMY 8:10–18

[10] When you have eaten and are satisfied, praise the LORD your God for the good land he has given you. [11] Be careful that you do not forget the LORD your God, failing to observe his commands, his laws and his decrees that I am giving you this day. [12] Otherwise, when you eat and are satisfied, when you build fine houses and settle down, [13] and when your herds and flocks grow large and your silver and gold increase and all you have is multiplied, [14] then your heart will become proud and you will forget the LORD your God, who brought you out of Egypt, out of the land of slavery. [15] He led you through the vast and dreadful desert, that thirsty and waterless land, with its venomous snakes and scorpions. He brought you water out of hard rock. [16] He gave you manna to eat

in the desert, something your fathers had never known, to humble and to test you so that in the end it might go well with you. [17] You may say to yourself, "My power and the strength of my hands have produced this wealth for me." [18] But remember the LORD your God, for it is he who gives you the ability to produce wealth, and so confirms his covenant, which he swore to your forefathers, as it is today.

## MATTHEW 25:14–30

[14] "Again, it will be like a man going on a journey, who called his servants and entrusted his property to them. [15] To one he gave five talents of money, to another two talents, and to another one talent, each according to his ability. Then he went on his journey. [16] The man who had received the five talents went at once and put his money to work and gained five more. [17] So also, the one with the two talents gained two more. [18] But the man who had received the one talent went off, dug a hole in the ground and hid his master's money. [19] "After a long time the master of those servants returned and settled accounts with them. [20] The man who had received the five talents brought the other five. 'Master,' he said, 'you entrusted me with five talents. See, I have gained five more.' [21] "His master replied, 'Well done, good and faithful servant! You have been faithful with a few things; I will put you in charge of many things. Come and share your master's happiness!' [22] "The man with the two talents also came. 'Master,' he said, 'you entrusted me with two talents; see, I have gained two more.' [23] "His master replied, 'Well done, good and faithful servant! You have been faithful with a few things; I will put you in charge of many things. Come and share your master's happiness!' [24] "Then the man who had received the one talent came. 'Master,' he said, 'I knew that you are a hard man, harvesting where you have not sown and gathering where you have not scattered seed. [25] So I was afraid and went out and hid your talent in the ground. See, here is what belongs to you.' [26] "His master replied, 'You wicked, lazy servant! So you knew that I harvest where I have not sown and gather where I have not scattered seed? [27] Well then, you should

> have put my money on deposit with the bankers, so that when I returned I would have received it back with interest. [28] " 'Take the talent from him and give it to the one who has the ten talents. [29] For everyone who has will be given more, and he will have an abundance. Whoever does not have, even what he has will be taken from him. [30] And throw that worthless servant outside, into the darkness, where there will be weeping and gnashing of teeth.'

## Preparing for Farewell (Deuteronomy 8:10–18)

Some would argue that the entire book of Deuteronomy is Moses' farewell speech. Moses was preparing the people for the land God had promised them. Moses had been their leader for more than forty years. He would not lead them into the Promised Land, but felt compelled to prepare them to receive the gift. The section of his speech in Deuteronomy 8:10–18 described the proper attitude toward the material blessings that the people would receive. The overall theme was "Don't ever forget God." However, within that overarching theme, Moses predicted many pitfalls and potential detours to their success in the Promised Land.

Moses believed the key to success was an intimate relationship with God through the observance of the law (Deut. 8:6). He warned the people that material success could cause them to lose sight of this priority. This part of Moses' speech can be divided into four sections: (1) A call to always remember God (v.10–11); (2) A warning of how easy it is to forget God (v.12–14); (3) The key to remembering God (v.15–16); and (4) the theological foundation for an approach to material wealth (v.17–18).

## A Call to Remember God (8:10–11)

Moses emphasized the theme of his entire farewell speech: Success is found only in a relationship with God. God had delivered the children of Israel from Egyptian slavery. God had provided for them in the wilderness. And now, God was going to give them the Promised Land.

Everything about the Hebrew experience had been centered on their relationship with God. Moses had delivered the law of God to the people. He wanted to be sure they would never forget God's law.

## A Warning of How Easy it is to Forget God (8:12–14)

Moses also spoke of the consequences of ignoring God's law. The law was designed to constantly draw the people's thoughts and hearts back toward God. Without the law the people would easily be drawn to themselves and begin to see their success as a product of their own efforts.

Moses described the process by which the people would be led astray. The people would eat until they were satisfied. This was in stark contrast to the wilderness years where they were given just enough food for daily subsistence. In the Promised Land they would have plenty of food. They would also build fine houses. This was another thing that was impossible during the wilderness years. Moses told them that in the Promised Land, for the first time in centuries, they would be able to build permanent, luxurious homes. They would be able to "settle down." Again, this was something they were not able to do in the desert. They had lived a nomadic lifestyle, constantly in search of water and better grazing land.

Moses warned them that in this new, more stable lifestyle, their flocks and herds would increase and their finances would grow. This was a sign of the ability to store, sell, and trade cattle, crops, and other goods. Moses was describing a shift from a nomadic, foraging culture, to a more stable, agri-business culture. And he was warning them that in the cultural transition it would be easy to forget God. Their hearts would grow proud of all they accumulated, and they would forget that it was God who had made it all possible.

## The Key to Remembering God (8:15–16)

Moses then launched into a recitation of what God had done for them. God had brought them out of slavery in the land of Egypt. God had led them through the wilderness regions of the Sinai, protecting them from all the hardships of that expansive and lifeless land. God had protected them from poisonous snakes and scorpions. God had given them water out of rocks. God had provided manna and quail on a daily basis. All of this had been provided by God so that his people would survive and prosper.

Through these hardships the Hebrew people had much to be thankful for. After centuries of slavery and an entire generation of existence in the wilderness, it had been a long and difficult journey for them to finally experience comfort and plenty. Moses warned them a grave danger inherent to comfort and luxury. The greatest danger was that they might be tempted to say, "My power and the strength of my hands have produced this wealth for me" (Deut. 8:17). There is a smug and unfounded confidence that can come with affluence. It is difficult to abandon yourself to complete trust in God when you go through life with so many financial and material safety nets. Eventually, God seems to be unnecessary.

## The Theological Foundation for Material Wealth (8:18)

Moses offered an important contrast from the thought patterns of verse 17 in the exhortation of verse 18. There can be a great temptation to believe that you are a self-made person, which stands in contrast to the theological truth that everything comes from God, including your ability to produce wealth. ". . .the world is mine, and all that is in it," says God (Psalm 50:12). He is the God who owns "the cattle on a thousand hills" (Ps. 50:9).

God provided both escape from Egypt and provision in the wilderness, not because the Hebrew people deserved it, but to keep them humble and spiritually prosperous (Deut. 8:16). They received manna and quail on a daily basis in order that they might be humbled by God's generosity; maintaining their exclusive dependence on God and growing prosperous in character and spiritual insight.

The biblical perspective on all things material is that everything belongs to God. Private ownership is a figment of our imagination. It is a false human construct designed to facilitate the consolidation of power. This concept was central to ancient Hebrew thought. It impacted the way they viewed cattle, crops, houses, family, and land. All of it was given to them by God as a stewardship.

# A BIBLICAL TALENT

The talent was one of several ancient units of mass, usually used to measure precious metal. It was approximately the mass of the water required to fill an amphora. An amphora was a ceramic jar used for the storage of various products, including wine.[2] A Greek, or Attic talent, was 26 kilograms, a Roman talent was 32.3 kilograms, an Egyptian talent was 27 kilograms, and a Babylonian talent was 30.3 kilograms.[3]

In the New Testament the talent as a unit of value would have been the heavy common talent and weighed about eighty pounds. This would have been worth approximately 6,000 denaraii. The denaraii was the average wage for a day of labor. One talent, therefore would be worth approximately twenty years of a day laborer's work. This makes the talent quite valuable, and so even the slave who received one talent clearly was given a huge amount of money.

The Parable of the Talents is the origin of the sense of the word "talent" meaning "gift or skill" as used in English and other languages. It came to denote anything of great value, including trade skills and artistic abilities.

## The Parable of the Talents (Matthew 25:14–30)

Jesus told a parable that affirmed this essential biblical truth. The Parable of the Talents is set in the larger discussion of Jesus' return and the coming kingdom of God. It spoke to what we should do with our God-given resources as we await Jesus' return. It also affirmed that everything belongs to God, and is given to us as a sober stewardship. The ultimate goal of this stewardship is to be a blessing to God, and others.

A wealthy man was going on a long journey. He decided to leave a total of eight talents to his most trusted servants. To one servant he left five talents, to another he left two, and to the final servant he left one. The inequality in amounts was in direct proportion to the abilities of each servant. One talent was equal to approximately twenty years of a day laborer's wage. This was a large amount of money and a significant

## Counting Your Blessings and Making Your Blessings Count

- Make a list of the ways that God has blessed you today. Develop a prayer of thanksgiving for each blessing.

- Name some things that you typically spend money on, but could do without. How much money could you save? Give that money to God.

- Make a list of the ways you might multiply what God has given you. At least half the list should be non-financial.

- Do something to serve God that takes you outside of your comfort zone and requires risk.

stewardship responsibility was placed on each servant. Servants were often used as managers and household administrators. A ruler's servants were sometimes the most trusted members of his family.

There is some debate over the actual meaning of the talents. The debate is mostly irrelevant to the ultimate meaning of the parable. Whether the talents are taken to signify financial wealth, character traits, giftedness, abilities, or time allotted on earth, it makes little difference. The point is the same: Whatever valuable resources God has entrusted to you, they belong to him, and he has given them to you to use for his honor and glory.

There were no instructions from the master as to what the servants were to do with the monies. However, there were two important aspects to the role of the steward. There was: (1) an entrusting, and (2) an accounting. The master entrusted each servant with a certain amount of his wealth. When the master returned, he held each servant accountable for the portion of the wealth entrusted to them.

The first two servants seemed to have grasped this concept. They immediately put the investment to work, doubling their master's money. The third servant, however, did nothing but hide the money. He admitted later that this was due to his fear of losing it. Others have speculated that everything from laziness to ignorance to a lack of abilities to procrastination kept him from investing wisely. He was, after all, the servant in whom the master had the least amount of confidence (having given him only one talent).

When the master returned, all three servants were held to the same standard. The first two showed that they had doubled the master's money and were rewarded. The reward was two-fold: (1) they would, in the future, be entrusted with even more in the master's kingdom, and (2) they would share in the master's happiness. What counts is not how much we start with, but what we do with what God has entrusted to us. The greatest reward, however, was to see the smile on the master's face, hear his words of praise, "Well done, good and faithful servant" (Matt. 25:21), and share in his joy. Even more fulfilling than added responsibility is the knowledge that our actions have been pleasing to God.

The third servant, however, had nothing to give the master but the principal investment. The master's anger was intense and his punishment swift. The servant's excuses were no saving grace. The master made it clear that we are not to ignore, abuse, or waste what we have been given from the Lord. To do so is tantamount to rebellion (Matt.25:24–30).

## Implications and Actions

The Parable of the Talents, coupled with Moses' warnings in his farewell speech (Deuteronomy 8:10–18), reveal the important biblical foundations for our attitude towards material wealth. The Scripture reveals four theological truths: (1) Everything belongs to God; (2) God entrusts us with a certain amount of his resources; (3) We are responsible to use and develop the resources God gives us; and (4) God will hold us accountable for the management of his resources.

These biblical concepts call us to take stock of the way we spend money, care for the environment, and use our time and natural talents. We should carefully analyze how we are investing God's resources. We should make an effort to leverage everything we have to bring God glory and further his plan for our world. In the end, God will reward us for our faithful stewardship of his resources.

## QUESTIONS

1. Have you developed a philosophy of money? If so, what is it? If not, what is stopping you from doing so?

2. How often do you analyze where your money is being spent, and why?

3. In what ways do you enjoy serving God? How often do you serve him?

4. How do you spend most of your time? What percentage of your time goes to serving God? How could you increase it?

5. What are some things you can do to invest in and care for God's creation?

## NOTES

1. Elizabeth Dunn and Michael Horton, "How to Buy Happiness," *Los Angeles Times,* May 19, 2013.

2. Allen C. Myers, ed., *The Eerdman's Bible Dictionary* (Grand Rapids Michigan, Eerdman's Publishing Co., 1987), 982.

3. Talent (Measurement)," Wikipedia, last modified July 23, 2013, http://en.wikipedia.org/wiki/Talent_(measurement) .

**FOCAL TEXTS**
Psalm 103; Luke 17:11–19

**BACKGROUND**
Psalm 103; Luke 17:11–19

**MAIN IDEA**
Disciples regularly express
their thankfulness to
God and others.

**QUESTION TO EXPLORE**
Do I regularly express
thankfulness to God
and others?

**STUDY AIM**
To decide how I will express
thankfulness to God and to
another person this week

**QUICK READ**
Thankfulness expressed to
God and others reveals a heart
of gratitude that produces
and receives blessings.

# LESSON TWELVE
## *Thankfulness*

## Introduction

Have you ever pulled out an old photo album and admired the images of days gone by? It could be pictures from your wedding day or the day you graduated from college. Maybe it's a snapshot of you standing by your first car or your high school prom picture with your sweetheart. These moments in our lives bring back fond memories and cause us to rejoice all over again with a sense of gratitude. That is exactly what David did in Psalm 103. He brought back images of days when God's grace had impacted his life. This caused David to thank God through an exuberant hymn of praise and sets an example for us as we express our thankfulness to God.

On the other hand, do you have memories of times when you failed to express thankfulness for God's blessings? Have you been tempted to take his blessings for granted? Jesus' encounter with ten lepers reveals a surprising example of someone who chose gratitude over presumption.

# PSALM 103

[1] Praise the LORD, O my soul; all my inmost being, praise his holy name. [2] Praise the LORD, O my soul, and forget not all his benefits— [3] who forgives all your sins and heals all your diseases, [4] who redeems your life from the pit and crowns you with love and compassion, [5] who satisfies your desires with good things so that your youth is renewed like the eagle's. [6] The LORD works righteousness and justice for all the oppressed. [7] He made known his ways to Moses, his deeds to the people of Israel: [8] The LORD is compassionate and gracious, slow to anger, abounding in love. [9] He will not always accuse, nor will he harbor his anger forever; [10] he does not treat us as our sins deserve or repay us according to our iniquities. [11] For as high as the heavens are above the earth, so great is his love for those who fear him; [12] as far as the east is from the west, so far has he removed our transgressions from us. [13] As a father has compassion on his children, so the LORD has compassion on those who fear him; [14] for he knows how we are formed, he remembers that we are dust. [15] As for man, his days are like grass, he flourishes like a flower of the field; [16] the wind blows over it

and it is gone, and its place remembers it no more. [17] But from everlasting to everlasting the LORD's love is with those who fear him, and his righteousness with their children's children— [18] with those who keep his covenant and remember to obey his precepts. [19] The LORD has established his throne in heaven, and his kingdom rules over all. [20] Praise the LORD, you his angels, you mighty ones who do his bidding, who obey his word. [21]Praise the LORD, all his heavenly hosts, you his servants who do his will. [22] Praise the LORD, all his works everywhere in his dominion. Praise the LORD, O my soul.

# LUKE 17:11–19

[11] Now on his way to Jerusalem, Jesus traveled along the border between Samaria and Galilee.[12] As he was going into a village, ten men who had leprosy met him. They stood at a distance [13] and called out in a loud voice, "Jesus, Master, have pity on us!" [14] When he saw them, he said, "Go, show yourselves to the priests." And as they went, they were cleansed. [15] One of them, when he saw he was healed, came back, praising God in a loud voice. [16] He threw himself at Jesus' feet and thanked him—and he was a Samaritan. [17] Jesus asked, "Were not all ten cleansed? Where are the other nine? [18] Was no one found to return and give praise to God except this foreigner?" [19] Then he said to him, "Rise and go; your faith has made you well."

## A Command to Praise God (Psalm 103:1–2)

Psalm 103 is a hymn of praise ascribed to the pen of King David. As with most of the hymns David wrote, the content is highly reflective. Psalm 103 begins a group of Psalms (103–106) that comprise a section of hymns that close Book 4 of the Psalms (90–106). The uniqueness of this group of psalms is that each of them begins with a command. Psalm 104:1 repeats the same stanza from the beginning of Psalm 103 when it says, "Praise the Lord, O my soul." Psalm 105 begins with, "Give thanks to the Lord." Finally, the beginning of Psalm 106 simply states, "Praise the Lord."

David declares, "Praise the Lord, O my soul; all my inmost being, praise his holy name" (Ps. 103:1). He repeats the command in verse 2 and adds the phrase "and forget not all his benefits." This stanza is repeated at the close of the psalm. For David, God's praise was a priority in his life. So much so that David wrote this psalm to himself. With the inclusion of the words "my soul," David made this psalm immensely personal. His example here is that we should praise God with our entire being. Everything in us should praise the Lord. Notably there are no petitions in this psalm, only praise and thanksgiving. As Christians, we should praise God with a sincerity that does not always include a "laundry list" of things we want him to do for us. Spiritual growth occurs when we take time to praise God for what he has already done.

An example of this is when David writes in verse 2 ". . .and forget not all his benefits." He goes on to list several attributes of God that give us reasons to praise and thank him. David reflected on who God was to him. He then described his encounters with God where he was the personal recipient of providential grace.

## Compelling Reasons to Give God Praise (103:3–5)

In verses 3–5, David listed five benefits from God that should command every Christian's thankfulness. Verse 3 says, ". . .who forgives all your sins and heals all your diseases." Here David intentionally linked forgiveness and healing. During David's time certain diseases such as leprosy and other physical ailments were thought to be linked to the presence of sin in one's life. Jesus later dispelled this notion (see John 9:3).

In order for us to be truly whole, we need God's healing of our bodies as well as his forgiveness of our sins; which brings healing to our souls. David wrote in verse 4: "who redeems your life from the pit and crowns you with love and compassion." David often reflected on the kindness of God shown to him in times of distress. To redeem can also be translated "to rescue." Some scholars suggest that this psalm was written while David was in some sort of trouble where only God could rescue him.

Finally, David said in verse 5 that God is the one "who satisfies your desires with good things so that your youth is renewed like the eagles." The word used here for "satisfies" literally means "to be filled with food." Therefore the "good things" that are mentioned here represent the mass amount of royal delicacies that were put before a king for his enjoyment and nourishment. This feasting is a metaphorical representation of enjoying a fulfilling life. It is awesome to know that we serve a God who is not only concerned about our spiritual well-being but is also interested in our overall enjoyment of life—another of God's blessings that can evoke our worship.

The eagle, throughout the Bible, is a symbol of freedom and youthful strength (Isaiah 40:31). Just as an eagle feasts on the food nature provides and then is strengthened to soar long distances, so also God provides us spiritual food, his word, which allows us to gain strength to soar above our troubles. Notice the verb tense of the Hebrew words for forgives, heals, redeems, crowns, and satisfies. Each of them represents an action of the past that can be carried forward to the present and into the future. In other words, David is thankful that God's forgiveness, healing, redemption, and satisfaction are ongoing as we continue to walk with him.

## Judge, Shepherd, and Father (103:6–14)

In verse six, David makes a transition and expounds more in-depth upon the mercy of God. Throughout the Psalms, God's justice is often contrasted with his mercy to illustrate two facets of God's love for his creation. In this section, David presents us with three images of God: a righteous judge, a watchful shepherd, and a loving father.

As a righteous judge (described in verse 6) we see God as being the one who "works righteousness and justice for all the oppressed." David then provides us with a contrasting view of God in verse 8 when he adds that "The Lord is compassionate and gracious, slow to anger, abounding in love."

Next we see God as a shepherd who leads and watches over his flock. Verse 7 says, "He made known his ways to Moses, his deeds to the people of Israel." David wrote this section of the psalm as a memory of the days when God led the children of Israel out of Egypt, through the wilderness, and into the Promised Land.

Lastly, God is described as a Father who "has compassion on his children" (103:13). The word translated "compassion" literally means "to show love with a deep sense of pity." This teaches us that God loves us like a father or a mother loves their children. It is love in its most profound form, almost immeasurable. God our Father not only pities us but he "knows" us. This word is often used in the Bible to describe God's intimate knowledge of his creation. He knows how he made us. Verse 14 tells us that ". . .he knows how we are formed, he remembers that we are dust." He is fully aware of our human limitations.

## The Final Chorus (103:15–22)

In the final section of this psalm, David contrasted man's transience with the permanence of God's covenantal love for his children. In verses 15–19, he compares the span of our lives with grass and the flowers of the field. As God's creation, our time on earth is temporary. The springing up and dying of the grass and the flowers are metaphorically used to portray our life on earth as brief, especially when compared to God's eternal love.

David closes the psalm the same way he started it, with a strong exhortation to "Praise the Lord." Three times he repeats this command, with the fourth being a refrain from the opening verse of the hymn. These hymns were also used as teaching psalms. David's thankfulness reminds us to never lose sight of the reasons we have for giving praise to the Lord.

## A Cry for Mercy (Luke 17:11–13)

The story of the ten lepers is as much about giving thanks to God as it is about receiving the miracle of God's healing power. In this episode, Jesus demonstrated that God's grace is available to all. Even the most despised social outcast is a candidate to receive God's mercy.

Jesus was on his way to Jerusalem and his journey took him along the border of Samaria and Galilee. As he entered an unnamed village he was met by ten leprous men who, as verse 12 describes, "stood at a distance." Leprosy was the most dreaded skin disease of Jesus' time. It was a contagious disease. Thus the Levitical law required that lepers were to be deemed "unclean." Therefore they could not reside in normal society but were sentenced to live the rest of their lives outside the city walls, away from the public, and separated from family and friends. These

## "GO, SHOW YOURSELVES TO THE PRIESTS"

There was typically only one occasion when a leper would have had contact with a priest: the moment he was designated as a leper after having contracted the disease. In order to see the priest again, the leper had to be fully convinced of his healing. The Levitical law required that a leper who was completely healed to show proof of his healing to the priest. Notice that Jesus did not heal the lepers and then send them to the priests. He sent them first. Their healing came as a result of their faith. The priests would confirm their healing and offer the sacrifices that were commanded by Moses (Leviticus 14); and then pronounce them clean. This would give the healed lepers the right to re-enter the village and be reunited with their families. This would call for a tremendous time of celebration, similar to the story of the killing of the fatted calf when the Prodigal Son returned home in Luke 15:23–24.

were law-abiding lepers who stood the proper distance (a minimum of six feet away) from Jesus.

Obviously these men knew who Jesus was and had heard about his healing power. They did not want to miss this opportunity. Verse 13 tells us, "they lifted up their voices and said, Jesus, Master, have pity on us!"

### Following Jesus' Instructions (17:14)

A similar story is found in 2 Kings 5:1–19 where Naaman, the Syrian commander who was himself a leper, entreated the prophet Elisha to heal him of his condition. In both cases, the lepers knew that nothing short of a miracle from God could cure them. Both of them were given instructions to follow, and a potential cure was subject to their faith and obedience to the instructions they received. For Naaman, his cure came as a result of bathing in the Jordan River seven times.

In the case of the ten lepers, Jesus showed compassion and instructed them to "Go, show yourselves to the priests" (Luke 17:14). The priests would then confirm their healing and pronounce them ceremonially clean. Faith is often expressed in our radical obedience to God's

---

## Growing in Thankfulness

Here are some suggestions for growing in your thankfulness.

- Cultivate an attitude of thankfulness in your daily and weekly worship.
- Practice beginning and ending each day with giving thanks to God.
- Periodically encourage family and friends to gather for a time of praise and testimony to the goodness of God.
- Trust God completely. Even in those moments when you don't fully understand his commands.

---

commands. All ten lepers received healing while in route to the priests. Their faith was exemplified in their actions. They had to believe that at some point between leaving Jesus and arriving at the priests, the miracle of healing would take place. This story provides an excellent example of how faith works. It is not enough to just believe. We have to put our faith into action.

### The Thankful Leper (17:15–19)

While all ten lepers were healed, only one returned to give thanks. Verse 15 states, "One of them, when he saw he was healed, came back, praising God in a loud voice. He threw himself at Jesus' feet and thanked him." Often this story is told with an emphasis on the nine who did not return. However, there was only one who sensed the need to show gratitude. The challenge of the text is that the majority of those who received the blessing were not thankful. The question we must ask ourselves is: Are we satisfied to be the recipients of God's grace without thanking him? As Christians, we should pause and show our gratitude to God every opportunity we get. 1 Thessalonians 5:18 says, "give thanks in all circumstances, for this is God's will for you in Christ Jesus."

In this passage the Gospel writer Luke chose to highlight the distinctiveness of one leper's lineage. He adds the commentary: ". . .and he was a Samaritan" (Luke 17:16). Since this episode takes place in the borderland between Samaria and Galilee, it is highly likely that this group of ten lepers would have been comprised of both Jews and Samaritans. The identification of this Samaritan leper was significant in that the Samaritans were not charged with the same worship customs as the Jews. Neither were they exposed to the culture of temple worship because the Samaritans were not allowed in the temple. In verses 17 and 18 when Jesus asks, "Where are the other nine?" he identifies this leper as a foreigner. The extraordinary faith of the Samaritan leper is seen in his willingness to return and worship God as he expressed thankfulness to Jesus for his healing.

In response to his act of perseverance and courage, Jesus rewarded the man with a second blessing. In verse 19 Jesus says to the former leper, "Rise and go; your faith has made you well." The word used for "well" in verse 19 is different from the word "cleansed" in verse 14. It carries with it the meaning of going beyond mere physical healing. The word describes the healing of the inner being of the soul. Some scholars argue that the language used in verse 19 indicates this leper received the additional blessing of his salvation after returning to give thanks.

## Implications and Actions

Thanksgiving should be a part of the lifestyle of every believer in Christ. Since the days when we were little toddlers we were taught to say "thank you" when someone gives us something or does something nice for us. God grants us his grace every day. When was the last time your prayers focused solely on praise for God's goodness? God desires our praise on a daily basis. Take a moment and think back over your life, the good times and the tough times. Certainly before the exercise is complete you will have a long list of things to thank God for. Let your gratitude be expressed outwardly in your praise to God.

## QUESTIONS

1. In Psalm 103:3–5, David provides a list of blessings he is thankful for. What are the things in your life that you are most thankful for?

2. How does thanksgiving impact your worship experience?

3. In what ways does the disease of leprosy compare to the effects of sin in our society?

4. Recall the moment you accepted Jesus Christ as your Lord and Savior. In what ways was your conversion experience similar to that of the Samaritan leper in Luke 17:15–19?

FOCAL TEXTS
Romans 10:8–15;
1 Corinthians 15:1–8

BACKGROUND
Romans 10:8–15;
1 Corinthians 15:1–8

MAIN IDEA
Disciples declare the
gospel of Jesus Christ.

QUESTION TO EXPLORE
Am I declaring the
gospel of Jesus Christ to
those who need him?

STUDY AIM
To commit to declaring
the gospel of Jesus
Christ to someone who
needs him this week

QUICK READ
The apostle Paul outlines
the content and the process
disciples can use to proclaim
the gospel of Jesus Christ.

# LESSON THIRTEEN
## *Witnessing*

## Introduction

An effective witness is like a signpost. It doesn't matter whether the sign is old or new, it has to be understandable and it has to point people in the right direction.[1] As Christians, we are witnesses to Jesus Christ. Our communication of the gospel must also be clear as we point the world to Jesus. When was the last time you pointed someone to Christ?

# ROMANS 10:8–15

[8] But what does it say? "The word is near you; it is in your mouth and in your heart," that is, the word of faith we are proclaiming: [9] That if you confess with your mouth, "Jesus is Lord," and believe in your heart that God raised him from the dead, you will be saved. [10] For it is with your heart that you believe and are justified, and it is with your mouth that you confess and are saved. [11] As the Scripture says, "Anyone who trusts in him will never be put to shame." [12] For there is no difference between Jew and Gentile—the same Lord is Lord of all and richly blesses all who call on him, [13] for, "Everyone who calls on the name of the Lord will be saved." [14] How, then, can they call on the one they have not believed in? And how can they believe in the one of whom they have not heard? And how can they hear without someone preaching to them? [15] And how can they preach unless they are sent? As it is written, "How beautiful are the feet of those who bring good news!"

# 1 CORINTHIANS 15:1–8

[1] Now, brothers, I want to remind you of the gospel I preached to you, which you received and on which you have taken your stand. [2] By this gospel you are saved, if you hold firmly to the word I preached to you. Otherwise, you have believed in vain. [3] For what I received I passed on to you as of first importance: that Christ died for our sins according to the Scriptures, [4] that he was buried, that he was raised on the third day according to the Scriptures, [5] and that he appeared to Peter, and then to the Twelve. [6] After

that, he appeared to more than five hundred of the brothers at the same time, most of whom are still living, though some have fallen asleep. ⁷ Then he appeared to James, then to all the apostles, ⁸ and last of all he appeared to me also, as to one abnormally born.

## Faith vs. the Law (Romans 10:8)

The law Israel received from God through Moses provided instruction for daily living. It also gave them a way to exercise righteousness before God. The law outlined everything they needed to know regarding worship and the holiness of God. However, the law was only a shadow of the revelation of the righteousness that is received by faith (as opposed to works) in Jesus Christ.

The comparison between faith and the law was what the apostle Paul sought to share with the Romans. Both the similarities and distinctions between the law given by Moses in the Old Testament, and the gospel of Jesus Christ in the New Testament, are made clear in this chapter. The justification Paul describes cannot be obtained by works or deeds, but by faith alone. Paul explained that the law brought blessings as a reward for the people's obedience to God, as well as curses if they disobeyed and turned away from him. We no longer have a list of laws to obey, but an opportunity to be completely justified before God and declared righteous by placing our faith and trust in Christ (Galatians 2:16).

In verse 8, Paul made a reference to Deuteronomy 30:14. He explained that Jesus is the "word of faith" that has fulfilled the law of Moses. Just as Moses and the children of Israel were required to love the Lord their God and keep his commandments in order to inherit blessings (Deut. 30:19–20), we must make a confession of faith in the Lord Jesus Christ and believe in our heart in order to inherit eternal life.

Paul pressed upon his Roman audience that, "the word is near you; it is in your mouth and in your heart" describing its closeness and availability. Paul went on to explain that it is as near and available now as it was in the Old Testament. Just as the children of Israel would publically express their belief and love for God through obedience to the law, we must now make a verbal confession of faith in Christ and believe in him with our hearts in order to receive life.

## The Proper Response to the Gospel (10:9–10)

Witnessing to the world and sharing our faith in Jesus Christ is one of the most important duties of Christians. When we seek to share the message of salvation in Jesus Christ, it is important that we communicate clearly what is needed for someone to authentically receive the gospel.

Placing one's faith in Christ is a personal decision, but it does require an open confession[2] with the mouth. Paul used the term "confess" in verse 9 which means "to say the same thing"[3.] This refers to the gospel message that Jesus Christ was crucified, that God raised him from the grave, and that he is Lord.

Paul also said in verse 10 that, "it is with the heart that you believe and are justified." The word translated "justified" in the Greek language means "to be made right with God." The two steps are simple and clear. One must confess with their mouth and believe in their heart in order to be saved. Believing in the heart is more than simply making an intellectual response to the gospel of Jesus Christ. The Greek word translated "believe" literally means "to be fully persuaded." Your clear and faithful witness and the convicting power of the Holy Spirit can work in tandem to bring about a sincere confession of faith in Christ.

The result of sincere confession and belief is that a person is "saved." They are rescued from the penalty of sin. They are saved *from something* (eternal separation from God), and they are saved *for something* (serving God through a growing relationship with Jesus Christ.)

## The Gospel is Trustworthy (10:11)

We live in a world where terms such as assurance, guarantee, proof, and reliability are significant when we decide to place our trust in something or someone. Paul assured the Romans that anyone who put their trust in God would not be put to shame. Because it is written in God's word, it is true. Paul referenced the prophecy found in Isaiah 28:16 concerning

## CASE STUDY

Victoria is a young, single mother in a local church. She attends church services sparingly. Though her manner of appearance is often provocative, her demeanor is usually quiet and reserved. Often times during the services she cries during the sermon but afterwards she's silent. Victoria is not a member of the church she attends.

Just before the invitation at the close of the worship service, when the pastor invites unbelievers to faith in Christ, she conveniently walks out of the service. She returns a week or two later and repeats the same pattern of behavior. This Sunday Victoria takes a seat next to you in the sanctuary. Are you willing to extend yourself toward Victoria today, or will you watch her exit the sanctuary? Would you be willing to set up a breakfast or lunch meeting with her to become better acquainted? What could you do to build a relationship with her that would lead to sharing the gospel?

the surety of souls who put their trust and belief in God. Isaiah refers to Jesus Christ as the "tested stone" or the "precious cornerstone" who would prove to be a sure foundation for anyone who places their trust in him.

## The Gospel is for Everyone (10:12–13)

Who can be saved? When Paul mentioned in verse 12 that, "there is no difference between Jew and Gentile," he was saying that the gospel is accessible to all of humanity. We are all guilty of sin because of our sin nature (Rom. 3:23). Paul taught that witnessing to sinners requires letting them know that regardless of who they are or what they've done, God's love and salvation are available to anyone who will receive it.

Paul assured the Romans that God is impartial with those who call on him. While we may make distinctions between people based on a diversity of cultures and ethnicities, Paul made it clear that the word of salvation does not discriminate; but is available to whoever puts their trust in Jesus. This is the beauty of the gospel: there is no partiality in it. It is available to young and old, rich and poor, law breakers and law abiding citizens, educated and uneducated; whoever calls upon the name of the lord shall be saved. Paul validates this with his restatement of the prophecy of Joel 2:32. Joel stood before Israel as they faced universal judgment and destruction due to their sin and disobedience. This is the picture of God rescuing every believer who puts their trust in him from eternal destruction.

## The Gospel Should be Shared by All Christians (10:14–15)

In this section, Paul argued that since there is no partiality for those who call on the name of the Lord, then everyone has the responsibility of spreading the message of the gospel of Jesus Christ. One might say, "I don't have a seminary education, or ministerial credentials." However, neither of these are prerequisites for spreading the gospel of Jesus Christ.

Paul made it clear that one cannot call upon a God he has not known or has not heard of. The same gospel message we heard and received has been given to us to spread throughout the world. It is important that we remember the process by which we were saved, which was through someone else sharing the message of the gospel with us. This challenges us to grow in our faith and to make every effort to express our faith in Christ through our daily lives.

Isaiah referred to the honor that is associated with those who carry the message of the gospel as ones having "beautiful feet" (Isaiah 52:7), and Paul quoted Isaiah in Romans 10:15. During Paul's time, people who proclaimed good news were called "heralds." A herald was someone who ran through town announcing (with a loud voice) the latest, most important news. Just like those heralds, we have been given the responsibility and authority to share the message of the gospel wherever we go.

## The Gospel Should be Shared in its Entirety (1 Corinthians 15:1–2)

Is the resurrection of the body literal or spiritual? In this chapter Paul addressed the need for the church at Corinth to return or to "hold firm" to their foundational beliefs concerning the gospel he had preached to them. False teaching had begun to creep into the church as a result of the influence of Greek culture, human philosophy, and a spirit of skepticism. These influences created doubt regarding the validity of the bodily resurrection of the Lord Jesus Christ. This issue presented some serious problems. The formation of sects and philosophical groups within the church had caused the believers to begin to question one of the foundational tenets of the Christian faith. It's interesting how a slight variation of the message of the gospel can be the difference between someone believing or rejecting its claims.

In verses 1–2, Paul does not seek to introduce a new teaching to challenge the skepticism concerning the bodily resurrection of Jesus. Instead, he exhorts his readers to "hold firmly" to the gospel he had preached to them so they would not be confused. In spite of the philosophical debates concerning the specifics of the gospel, he encouraged the Corinthians to focus on the foundational principles of the faith.

## The Basics of the Gospel of Jesus Christ (15:3–8)

Paul provides a four point outline of the message of the gospel of Jesus Christ. He began by reminding his readers that the gospel message he preached to them was the same message he received from Jesus (Galatians 1:12). He then outlines the gospel: **1) Christ died for our sins according to the Scriptures** (Psalm 16:10; Isaiah 53:8–10). While skeptics asserted that the resurrection never happened[4,] Paul argues in verse 4 that **2) Christ was buried,** which verified an authentic death. It is so important for us as disciples to know what we believe and why. As we share our faith in Jesus Christ we must be convinced that the message of the gospel is true and that it contains the power to change lives. **3) Jesus was raised on the third day** (a bodily resurrection), and **4) Jesus appeared to Peter first, then to the twelve, and then to numerous others including Paul; all according to the Scripture.**

There were eyewitnesses to the fact that Christ had indeed died, was buried, and was resurrected by God for the sins of the world. After his resurrection, Jesus appeared to more than five hundred witnesses. The words of Paul prove that the message of the gospel of Jesus Christ is true and had proven to be life-transforming for those who believed. Our commission as disciples is to proclaim our faith as we share the facts of the gospel (Matthew 28:18–20).

No event in history compares to the resurrection of Christ. The mention of Jesus' appearance to Peter, then to the twelve, and then to more than five hundred of the disciples at the same time proved to be verifiable facts for those who doubted Paul's words. Paul stated that many of the people who witnessed these things were still living. This meant they were able to bear witness to the resurrection. These post-resurrection appearances are direct evidence that Christ did indeed die, was buried, and was raised from the dead for our sins.

## Applying this Lesson to Life

Witnessing to those who need God's gift of salvation is vital for the world we live in. The gospel has the power to change lives forever. Paul provides for us the message and the motivation needed to be all that God has called us to be as disciples of Jesus Christ. The message Paul shared with the Roman Christians was that by faith in Christ we can be saved from sin and condemnation. Paul speaks clearly that the saving word of God is near and available to us.

The word of God has been fulfilled in the life, death, and resurrection of our Lord Jesus Christ. It has the power to change the life of anyone who puts their trust in him. The gospel is available to anyone who desires to receive it regardless of age, race, creed, color, sex, culture, economic status, or past failures. Therefore it is incumbent upon us as Christian disciples to witness to those who have not been exposed to the gospel of Jesus Christ. God himself has given us the authority and the means to impact the world with the love of Christ. Are you willing to commit to daily sharing the message of Jesus Christ with those you encounter?

## QUESTIONS

1. Are you regularly sharing the message of the gospel of Jesus Christ with those who need salvation? Who do you know who needs to hear the gospel?

2. By what authority do you have as a follower of Christ to share the message of the gospel? (see Matthew 28:18–20)

3. What are the basics of the gospel?

4. What biblical proof do we have that Christ was truly raised from the dead?

5. Is the message of the gospel of Jesus Christ for everyone? Does everyone have access to salvation?

6. What effect does the message of the gospel of Jesus Christ have on those who believe?

# NOTES

1. John White, *The Fight: A Practical Handbook for Christian Living* (Downers Grove, Illinois: InterVarsity Press, 1976), 75.

2. Romans 10:9 "Confess"—to declare openly by way of speaking out freely, such confession being the effect of deep conviction of facts—from W.E. Vine, Merrill F. Unger, William White, Jr., *Vine's Complete Expository Dictionary of Old and New Testament Words* (Nashville: Thomas Nelson Publishers, 1984).

3. Romans 10:9 "Confess" [homologeō] to say the same thing as another, i.e. to agree with, assent confession is made (*Strong's Talking Greek & Hebrew Dictionary*)

4. 1 Cor. 15 "Sadducees"- distinguishing doctrine of the Sadducees was the denial of man's resurrection after death—from William Smith, entry for "Sadducees", *Smith's Bible Dictionary*, 1901.

FOCAL TEXTS

Isaiah 6:1–8; Revelation 4:1–11

BACKGROUND

Isaiah 6:1–8; Revelation 4:1–11

MAIN IDEA

Disciples respond to God's revelation with a lifestyle of worship.

QUESTION TO EXPLORE

How can I respond to God's revelation with a lifestyle of worship?

STUDY AIM

To describe a lifestyle of worship and choose to respond to God's revelation in this manner

QUICK READ

A lifestyle of authentic worship begins with seeing God for who he truly is.

# LESSON FOURTEEN
## *Worship*

## Introduction

Eye exams are critical to keep the objects we see on a daily basis in focus. Our vision can become blurred if we neglect these routine exams. The replacement of old lenses with new ones can bring objects that were once hard to see into clear focus.

The children of Israel had lost their focus on God. The object of their worship had become material things instead of the God who creates all things. Sin had blurred their vision of God and they had failed to give him the worship he deserves. Isaiah's encounter with God brought into profound clarity his (and the nation of Israel's) sinfulness and God's holiness. His worship experience of awe, confession, and forgiveness was life-changing.

Likewise, John's glimpse into the throne room of heaven was an awe-inspiring revelation of the unending worship of the eternal God. These two encounters remind us of the magnificence and meaning of worship. Highly effective disciples respond to God's revelation by worshipping him with their lips and their lives.

# ISAIAH 6:1–8

[1] In the year that King Uzziah died, I saw the Lord seated on a throne, high and exalted, and the train of his robe filled the temple. [2] Above him were seraphs, each with six wings: With two wings they covered their faces, with two they covered their feet, and with two they were flying. [3] And they were calling to one another: "Holy, holy, holy is the LORD Almighty; the whole earth is full of his glory." [4] At the sound of their voices the doorposts and thresholds shook and the temple was filled with smoke. [5] "Woe to me!" I cried. "I am ruined! For I am a man of unclean lips, and I live among a people of unclean lips, and my eyes have seen the King, the LORD Almighty." [6] Then one of the seraphs flew to me with a live coal in his hand, which he had taken with tongs from the altar. [7] With it he touched my mouth and said, "See, this has touched your lips; your guilt is taken away and your sin atoned for." [8] Then I heard the voice of the Lord saying, "Whom shall I send? And who will go for us?" And I said, "Here am I. Send me!"

# REVELATION 4:1–11

¹ After this I looked, and there before me was a door standing open in heaven. And the voice I had first heard speaking to me like a trumpet said, "Come up here, and I will show you what must take place after this." ² At once I was in the Spirit, and there before me was a throne in heaven with someone sitting on it. ³ And the one who sat there had the appearance of jasper and carnelian. A rainbow, resembling an emerald, encircled the throne. ⁴ Surrounding the throne were twenty-four other thrones, and seated on them were twenty-four elders. They were dressed in white and had crowns of gold on their heads. ⁵ From the throne came flashes of lightning, rumblings and peals of thunder. Before the throne, seven lamps were blazing. These are the seven spirits of God. ⁶ Also before the throne there was what looked like a sea of glass, clear as crystal. In the center, around the throne, were four living creatures, and they were covered with eyes, in front and in back. ⁷ The first living creature was like a lion, the second was like an ox, the third had a face like a man, the fourth was like a flying eagle. ⁸ Each of the four living creatures had six wings and was covered with eyes all around, even under his wings. Day and night they never stop saying: "HOLY, HOLY, HOLY IS THE LORD GOD ALMIGHTY, WHO WAS, AND IS, AND IS TO COME." ⁹ Whenever the living creatures give glory, honor and thanks to him who sits on the throne and who lives for ever and ever, ¹⁰ the twenty-four elders fall down before him who sits on the throne, and worship him who lives for ever and ever. They lay their crowns before the throne and say: ¹¹ "You are worthy, our Lord and God, to receive glory and honor and power, for you created all things, and by your will they were created and have their being."

## God is on the Throne (Isaiah 6:1–4)

Isaiah dates this passage by informing us that the experience he is about to describe occurred in the year that King Uzziah died. Uzziah reigned as king in Jerusalem for fifty-two years and died about 740 B.C.

(2 Chronicles 26:3). Uzziah was a good king until he became powerful and eventually succumbed to pride. He attempted to burn incense on the altar of incense in the temple of the Lord. This task was to be performed by priests who were consecrated to perform this task. Uzziah was stricken with leprosy on his forehead because of his act of unfaithfulness and he died a leper.

What would the people do now that King Uzziah was dead? God provided the answer by giving Isaiah a peek into the throne room of heaven. Isaiah sees the true King of Israel high and lifted up in all of his glory. Isaiah does not see God's face as you and I would look upon the face of someone. We are reminded that no man has seen God at any time (John 1:18). Isaiah witnessed what true worship really means when he turned his attention to the seraphs. These were angelic beings mentioned only here in Isaiah. Isaiah does not tell us how many seraphs were present.

Each seraph had six wings which were used to cover their eyes and feet and to fly. They covered their eyes to demonstrate their unworthiness to gaze upon the glory of God. They were of one accord in their worship of God as they cried out "Holy, holy, holy is the Lord Almighty" (6:3). Their focus and attention were directed to God and God alone. This is the same lifestyle of worship that God requires of us.

## WORD STUDY

Seraphim—These are an order of heavenly beings mentioned in Isaiah 6:2–3. The word *seraph* has been defined as "bright" or "shining", but the verb *seraph* means "to burn." The root meaning has the transitive sense of "consuming with fire" (as when it is used adjectively of the "fiery" serpents of Numbers 21:6), as opposed to "glowing with heat." Each seraph had a face, hands, and feet, indicating they are not merely mystical beings, but are possessed of powers which are used to do God's will. Each has three pairs of wings, one pair being used to veil their faces (as being unworthy to look on God); another pair was used to cover their feet (as being in an attitude of waiting upon God to carry out his behests); and the third pair was used for flight (the rapid activity of fulfilling that for which they were sent.) Thus they differ from the cherubim in Ezekiel 10, and the living creatures in Revelation 4:8.[1]

## Isaiah Realizes His Sinful Condition (6:5)

When we see God for who he truly is, we see ourselves for who we really are. Even at our best, Isaiah says that all our righteous acts are like filthy rags (64:6). Isaiah pronounced judgment upon himself as a man condemned by unclean lips. He turned the spotlight on himself first before stating that he also lived among a people in the same sinful condition. Jesus taught in the Gospel of Matthew that we must first take the plank out of our own eye before we can remove the speck from our brother's eye (Matthew 7:3–5). Our sinfulness should result in our destruction, but we are not consumed because of God's grace. Such grace should motivate us to embrace a lifestyle of worship.

## The Cleansing Grace of God (6:6–7)

After confessing his sinful condition, Isaiah was prepared to receive the grace of God. It is only at the point of confession that we can receive grace from the hand of God. God initiated the process to cleanse Isaiah by dispatching a seraph to the altar to retrieve a live coal. The seraph was not careless in the approach taken to remove the coal from the altar. The altar represented the place of atonement. The seraph used tongs to remove the live coal because it represented a holy thing. The seraph placed the coal in his hand and touched the mouth of Isaiah. Immediately his guilt was removed and his sin atoned for.

## The Great Invitation (6:8)

After being cleansed from his sinful condition, Isaiah was ready to serve the Lord. God once again initiated the action by way of a question. "Whom shall I send? And who will go for us?" The "us" points to the plurality of the Godhead. The plurality of the Godhead can be seen at the baptism of Jesus by John the Baptist in the Jordan River. After Jesus came up out of the water, "heaven was opened, and he saw the Spirit of God descending like a dove and lighting on him. And a voice from heaven said, 'This is my Son, whom I love; with him I am well pleased'" (Matthew 3:16–17).

---

## CASE STUDY

John is the CEO of a fortune 500 company. He is married with two children. John is a workaholic and spends most of his weekends coaching little league soccer and fishing. He goes to church when not busy with these activities, but has never committed his life to Christ. His wife and children are actively involved in the life of their local church and rarely miss a worship service.

John grew up in a home where no one worshipped God and he feels the time he "puts in" at church is great, especially compared to the environment he grew up in. John is your best friend and you are concerned about his relationship with God. How would you approach John and explain to him the kind of lifestyle God is looking for?

---

Isaiah accepted the great invitation and declared, "Here am I. Send me!" The invitation was not addressed to a specific person. God will not demand service from anyone who does not give it voluntarily. God is still calling people to go for him. Jesus said, "The harvest is plentiful, but the workers are few" (Matt. 9:37).

## Another Glimpse of the Throne Room of Heaven (Revelation 4:1–7)

John takes us into the throne room of heaven and describes to us things that the human mind can't fully comprehend. The One who invites him is none other than Jesus Christ, whose voice is described like that of a trumpet in chapter one of Revelation. John's attention is immediately drawn to a throne. The glory that flows from the throne is described as an array of brilliant colors. God is so holy that John was not able to see him as he really is. God is described as living in "unapproachable light, whom no one has seen or can see" (1 Timothy 6:16). The rainbow John mentions is representative of God's grace to humanity. God made a promise to Noah that the world would never be destroyed again by a flood (Genesis 9:12–15).

The throne is surrounded by twenty-four other thrones with twenty-four elders seated on them. The twenty-four elders may refer to the twelve tribes of Israel and the twelve apostles of Jesus. The new Jerusalem is described as a city having twelve gates and twelve foundations. The names of the twelve tribes of the children of Israel are written on the gates and the names of the twelve apostles are written on the foundations (Revelation 21:12–14).

The elders were dressed in white, which is a symbol of purity. The crowns of gold represented the honor conferred upon them, similar to those who receive the highest honor of a gold medal in the Olympics. The gold crowns represented that which is not corrupt or subject to tarnish.

Millions have witnessed spectacular fireworks on the Fourth of July. We are captivated by the sights and sounds of bottle rockets exploding in mid-air. These exhibits are nothing when compared to the majesty and power coming from the throne of God (Rev. 4:5). This is the same God who revealed himself to Moses on Mount Sinai in a similar fashion (Exodus 20:18).

Four living creatures surrounded the throne of God. These were angelic beings that guard the throne and lead the praise and worship of God. They have eyes over their entire being and nothing escapes their view. These living creatures were described in the vision of Ezekiel by the Kebar River (Ezekiel 1:10). The first living creature was like a lion; the strongest of the wild beasts. The second was like an ox; the strongest of domesticated animals. The third had the face of a man; the one whom God gave authority to rule over his creation. The fourth was like a flying eagle; the greatest bird of the air.

## Praise Ye the Lord (4:8–11)

The four living creatures lead in a chorus of praise and worship. With the fruit of their lips they begin a never-ending chorus of giving honor and glory to the One who sits on the throne. Day and night they give praise to the God of all creation. God is looking for people who will worship him seven-days-a-week, not just on Sunday. The four living creatures ascribe glory to his name by repeating the refrain of "Holy, holy, holy." Isaiah reported this same refrain when he described his vision of the Lord lifted high and exalted in the temple.

The four living creatures declared the eternity of God with the words, "who was, and is, and is to come" (4:8). There is no beginning or ending with God. He is the Alpha and Omega. At the sight of the four living creatures leading worship, the twenty-four elders fell down before the throne and joined in worship. They fall down as a sign of humility and adoration of the One who lives forever and ever. As an act of worship they lay their crowns before the throne to signify that God and God alone is worthy to be praised. God is worthy because he created all things.

## Application for Life

Life is filled with distractions. Often things get in our way that prevent us from achieving our goals. Some distractions are self-inflicted, while others arise from external forces. A co-worker prevents you from completing a work assignment by engaging you in meaningless conversation. You fail to complete a homework assignment because you choose to watch television instead. God desires for us to have an authentic worship experience with him on a daily basis. Are there distractions you need to remove from your life in order to experience times of authentic worship with God? Will you respond to God's revelation to you with a lifestyle of worship?

## QUESTIONS

1. How do you think the people of Israel would have responded if they had experienced Isaiah's vision of heaven for themselves?

2. What connection do you see between the experiences of John and Isaiah related to worship?

3. How would you compare your lifestyle of worship to the worship that God demands?

4. What changes do you need to make to reflect a lifestyle of
   authentic worship? How will you bring those changes about?

NOTES ────────────────────────────────────────────

1. W.E. Vine, Merrill F. Unger, William White, Jr., *Vine's Expository Dictionary of Old and New Testament Words* (Nashville: Thomas Nelson Publishers, 1996), 124–125.

# Our Next New Study
(Available for use beginning September 2014)

## LETTERS TO THE
## EPHESIANS AND TIMOTHY:
## Guidance for the Church and Its Leaders

# How to Order More Bible Study Materials

It's easy! Just fill in the following information. For additional Bible study materials available both in print and online, see www.baptistwaypress.org, or get a complete order form of available print materials—including Spanish materials—by calling 1-866-249-1799 or e-mailing baptistway@texasbaptists.org.

| Title of item | Price | Quantity | Cost |
|---|---|---|---|
| **This Issue:** | | | |
| 14 Habits of Highly Effective Disciples—Study Guide (BWP001177) | $3.95 | _____ | _____ |
| 14 Habits of Highly Effective Disciples—Large Print Study Guide (BWP001178) | $4.25 | _____ | _____ |
| 14 Habits of Highly Effective Disciples—Teaching Guide (BWP001179) | $4.95 | _____ | _____ |
| **Additional Issues Available:** | | | |
| Growing Together in Christ—Study Guide (BWP001036) | $3.25 | _____ | _____ |
| Growing Together in Christ—Teaching Guide (BWP001038) | $3.75 | _____ | _____ |
| Guidance for the Seasons of Life—Study Guide (BWP001157) | $3.95 | _____ | _____ |
| Guidance for the Seasons of Life—Large Print Study Guide (BWP001158) | $4.25 | _____ | _____ |
| Guidance for the Seasons of Life—Teaching Guide (BWP001159) | $4.95 | _____ | _____ |
| Living Generously for Jesus' Sake—Study Guide (BWP001137) | $3.95 | _____ | _____ |
| Living Generously for Jesus' Sake—Large Print Study Guide (BWP001138) | $4.25 | _____ | _____ |
| Living Generously for Jesus' Sake—Teaching Guide (BWP001139) | $4.95 | _____ | _____ |
| Living Faith in Daily Life—Study Guide (BWP001095) | $3.55 | _____ | _____ |
| Living Faith in Daily Life—Large Print Study Guide (BWP001096) | $3.95 | _____ | _____ |
| Living Faith in Daily Life—Teaching Guide (BWP001097) | $4.25 | _____ | _____ |
| Participating in God's Mission—Study Guide (BWP001077) | $3.55 | _____ | _____ |
| Participating in God's Mission—Large Print Study Guide (BWP001078) | $3.95 | _____ | _____ |
| Participating in God's Mission—Teaching Guide (BWP001079) | $3.95 | _____ | _____ |
| Profiles in Character—Study Guide (BWP001112) | $3.55 | _____ | _____ |
| Profiles in Character—Large Print Study Guide (BWP001113) | $4.25 | _____ | _____ |
| Profiles in Character—Teaching Guide (BWP001114) | $4.95 | _____ | _____ |
| Genesis: People Relating to God—Study Guide (BWP001088) | $2.35 | _____ | _____ |
| Genesis: People Relating to God—Large Print Study Guide (BWP001089) | $2.75 | _____ | _____ |
| Genesis: People Relating to God—Teaching Guide (BWP001090) | $2.95 | _____ | _____ |
| Ezra, Haggai, Zechariah, Nehemiah, Malachi—Study Guide (BWP001071) | $3.25 | _____ | _____ |
| Ezra, Haggai, Zechariah, Nehemiah, Malachi—Large Print Study Guide (BWP001072) | $3.55 | _____ | _____ |
| Ezra, Haggai, Zechariah, Nehemiah, Malachi—Teaching Guide (BWP001073) | $3.75 | _____ | _____ |
| Psalms: Songs from the Heart of Faith—Study Guide (BWP001152) | $3.95 | _____ | _____ |
| Psalms: Songs from the Heart of Faith—Large Print Study Guide (BWP001153) | $4.25 | _____ | _____ |
| Psalms: Songs from the Heart of Faith—Teaching Guide (BWP001154) | $4.95 | _____ | _____ |
| Jeremiah and Ezekiel: Prophets of Judgment and Hope—Study Guide (BWP001172) | $3.95 | _____ | _____ |
| Jeremiah and Ezekiel: Prophets of Judgment and Hope—Large Print Study Guide (BWP001173) | $4.25 | _____ | _____ |
| Jeremiah and Ezekiel: Prophets of Judgment and Hope—Teaching Guide (BWP001174) | $4.95 | _____ | _____ |
| Amos. Hosea, Isaiah, Micah: Calling for Justice, Mercy, and Faithfulness—Study Guide (BWP001132) | $3.95 | _____ | _____ |
| Amos. Hosea, Isaiah, Micah: Calling for Justice, Mercy, and Faithfulness—Large Print Study Guide (BWP001133) | $4.25 | _____ | _____ |
| Amos. Hosea, Isaiah, Micah: Calling for Justice, Mercy, and Faithfulness—Teaching Guide (BWP001134) | $4.95 | _____ | _____ |
| The Gospel of Matthew: A Primer for Discipleship—Study Guide (BWP001127) | $3.95 | _____ | _____ |
| The Gospel of Matthew: A Primer for Discipleship—Large Print Study Guide (BWP001128) | $4.25 | _____ | _____ |
| The Gospel of Matthew: A Primer for Discipleship—Teaching Guide (BWP001129) | $4.95 | _____ | _____ |
| The Gospel of Mark: People Responding to Jesus—Study Guide (BWP001147) | $3.95 | _____ | _____ |
| The Gospel of Mark: People Responding to Jesus—Large Print Study Guide (BWP001148) | $4.25 | _____ | _____ |
| The Gospel of Mark: People Responding to Jesus—Teaching Guide (BWP001149) | $4.95 | _____ | _____ |
| The Gospel of Luke: Jesus' Personal Touch—Study Guide (BWP001167) | $3.95 | _____ | _____ |
| The Gospel of Luke: Jesus' Personal Touch—Large Print Study Guide (BWP001168) | $4.25 | _____ | _____ |
| The Gospel of Luke: Jesus' Personal Touch—Teaching Guide (BWP001169) | $4.95 | _____ | _____ |
| The Gospel of John: Light Overcoming Darkness, Part One—Study Guide (BWP001104) | $3.55 | _____ | _____ |
| The Gospel of John: Light Overcoming Darkness, Part One—Large Print Study Guide (BWP001105) | $3.95 | _____ | _____ |
| The Gospel of John: Light Overcoming Darkness, Part One—Teaching Guide (BWP001106) | $4.50 | _____ | _____ |
| The Gospel of John: Light Overcoming Darkness, Part Two—Study Guide (BWP001109) | $3.55 | _____ | _____ |
| The Gospel of John: Light Overcoming Darkness, Part Two—Large Print Study Guide (BWP001110) | $3.95 | _____ | _____ |
| The Gospel of John: Light Overcoming Darkness, Part Two—Teaching Guide (BWP001111) | $4.50 | _____ | _____ |

| | | | |
|---|---|---|---|
| The Book of Acts: Time to Act on Acts 1:8—Study Guide (BWP001142) | $3.95 | _____ | _____ |
| The Book of Acts: Time to Act on Acts 1:8—Large Print Study Guide (BWP001143) | $4.25 | _____ | _____ |
| The Book of Acts: Time to Act on Acts 1:8—Teaching Guide (BWP001144) | $4.95 | _____ | _____ |
| The Corinthian Letters—Study Guide (BWP001121) | $3.55 | _____ | _____ |
| The Corinthian Letters—Large Print Study Guide (BWP001122) | $4.25 | _____ | _____ |
| The Corinthian Letters—Teaching Guide (BWP001123) | $4.95 | _____ | _____ |
| Galatians and 1&2 Thessalonians—Study Guide (BWP001080) | $3.55 | _____ | _____ |
| Galatians and 1&2 Thessalonians—Large Print Study Guide (BWP001081) | $3.95 | _____ | _____ |
| Galatians and 1&2 Thessalonians—Teaching Guide (BWP001082) | $3.95 | _____ | _____ |
| Hebrews and the Letters of Peter—Study Guide (BWP001162) | $3.95 | _____ | _____ |
| Hebrews and the Letters of Peter—Large Print Study Guide (BWP001163) | $4.25 | _____ | _____ |
| Hebrews and the Letters of Peter—Teaching Guide (BWP001164) | $4.95 | _____ | _____ |
| Letters of James and John—Study Guide (BWP001101) | $3.55 | _____ | _____ |
| Letters of James and John—Large Print Study Guide (BWP001102) | $3.95 | _____ | _____ |
| Letters of James and John—Teaching Guide (BWP001103) | $4.25 | _____ | _____ |

## Coming for use beginning September 2014

| | | | |
|---|---|---|---|
| Letters to the Ephesians and Timothy—Study Guide (BWP001182) | $3.95 | _____ | _____ |
| Letters to the Ephesians and Timothy—Large Print Study Guide (BWP001183) | $4.25 | _____ | _____ |
| Letters to the Ephesians and Timothy—Teaching Guide (BWP001184) | $4.95 | _____ | _____ |

Cost
of items (Order value) _____

Shipping charges
(see chart*) _____

TOTAL _____

| Standard (UPS/Mail) Shipping Charges* | | | |
|---|---|---|---|
| Order Value | Shipping charge** | Order Value | Shipping charge** |
| $.01—$9.99 | $6.50 | $160.00—$199.99 | $24.00 |
| $10.00—$19.99 | $8.50 | $200.00—$249.99 | $28.00 |
| $20.00—$39.99 | $9.50 | $250.00—$299.99 | $30.00 |
| $40.00—$59.99 | $10.50 | $300.00—$349.99 | $34.00 |
| $60.00—$79.99 | $11.50 | $350.00—$399.99 | $42.00 |
| $80.00—$99.99 | $12.50 | $400.00—$499.99 | $50.00 |
| $100.00—$129.99 | $15.00 | $500.00—$599.99 | $60.00 |
| $130.00—$159.99 | $20.00 | $600.00—$799.99 | $72.00** |

*Please call 1-866-249-1799 if the exact amount is needed prior to ordering.

**For order values $800.00 and above, please call 1-866-249-1799 or check www.baptistwaypress.org

Please allow three weeks for standard delivery. For express shipping service: Call 1-866-249-1799 for information on additional charges.

YOUR NAME _____

PHONE _____

YOUR CHURCH _____

DATE ORDERED _____

SHIPPING ADDRESS _____

CITY _____

STATE _____ ZIP CODE _____

E-MAIL _____

**MAIL** this form with your check for the total amount to:
BAPTISTWAY PRESS, Baptist General Convention of Texas,
333 North Washington, Dallas, TX 75246-1798
(Make checks to "BaptistWay Press")

OR, **CALL** your order toll-free: 1-866-249-1799
(M-Fri 8:30 a.m.-5:00 p.m. central time).

OR, **E-MAIL** your order to: baptistway@texasbaptists.org.

OR, **ORDER ONLINE** at www.baptistwaypress.org.

We look forward to receiving your order! Thank you!